CARDINALS

Where Have You Gone?

ROB RAINS

www.SportsPublishingLLC.com

ISBN: 1-58261-155-6

Publishers: Peter L. Bannon and Joseph J. Bannon Sr.
Senior managing editor: Susan M. Moyer
Acquisitions editor: Mike Pearson
Developmental editor: Doug Hoepker
Art director: K. Jeffrey Higgerson
Book design: Jennifer L. Polson
Dust jacket design: Kenneth J. O'Brien
Project manager: Kathryn R. Holleman
Imaging: Kenneth J. O'Brien
Photo editor: Erin Linden-Levy
Vice president of sales and marketing: Kevin King
Media and promotions managers: Mike Hagan (regional),
        Randy Fouts (national), Maurey Williamson (print)

Printed in the United States of America

Sports Publishing L.L.C.
804 North Neil Street
Champaign, IL 61820

Phone: 1-877-424-2665
Fax: 217-363-2073
Web site: www.SportsPublishingLLC.com

This book is dedicated to all members of the Cardinals Family—the owners, the front office staff, the on-field staff, the players, everyone in the minor leagues, and most importantly, the fans. This might be the largest extended family in the world, all united by their love of Cardinal baseball.

CONTENTS

PREFACE

"Family" is a relative term. That is true, of course, in the literal sense. *Webster's* primary definition of the word is "a fundamental social group in society consisting especially of a man and woman and their offspring."

The added definitions include "a group of people sharing common ancestry" and "distinguished lineage."

These definitions all prove what many people have believed for a long time. The St. Louis Cardinals, and every player who has ever worn the birds on the bat uniform, or every person who ever worked for the team in any capacity, or any person who ever bought a T-shirt or a hat, or attended a game at Sportsman's Park or Busch Stadium, or who watched a game on television or listened to Jack Buck, Harry Caray or any of the other announcers on KMOX and the Cardinals radio network, are part of the Cardinal Family.

Like any family, the Cardinals' family has its patriarchs. Stan Musial, Bob Gibson, Lou Brock, Red Schoendienst and Ozzie Smith are currently in that class. Other greats have passed on, and many of the future stars have yet to be identified.

If you are lucky, like I was, you are born into the Cardinal Family. It is a birthright to be able to cheer for the Cardinals. The love of the team, and the game of baseball, is passed down from generation to generation just like the family Bible. There really is no doubt that Cardinal baseball is almost as sacrosanct as a religion.

I went to my first baseball game in 1964, at Sportsman's Park, to watch the Cardinals play the Milwaukee Braves. I was 8 years old, and my mother, brother and I made the trip by bus to St. Louis from our home in Springfield, Missouri. I remember no details about the game, except one very vivid memory. My favorite player was Ken Boyer. He didn't play that day. Phil Gagliano took his place at third base.

Nothing against Gagliano, but I was upset that Boyer didn't play. I know how kids who came to games in the late 1990s felt when Mark McGwire wasn't in the lineup, or kids this year will feel when

Albert Pujols doesn't play. We all understand that players have to get a day off now and then, but why does it have to be that particular day in which we are sitting in the stands?

Missing Boyer in action that day did not diminish my love for the Cardinals. When I played games in my backyard while listening to Buck and Caray on the radio, I became Brock and Gibson. Years later, I knew I would never be a candidate for the Cardinals' roster, but I was determined to stay connected with my team as I grew older.

Luckily, I was able to become a sportswriter, first for United Press International, then the *St. Louis Globe-Democrat*. My job was to cover the Cardinals. I had the thrill of covering the 1982 and 1985 championship teams on a daily basis. Even though we maintained a professional relationship, many players on those teams, and manager Whitey Herzog, became close personal friends. I am proud to say I still consider those players, as well as Whitey, my good friends.

I honestly believe I still would be covering the Cardinals on a daily basis today if the *Globe-Democrat* had not ceased publication on October 31, 1986. Gone was the only job I truly ever wanted in my life. As a Christian, however, I honestly believe the saying that when God closes a door, He opens a window.

That window opened for me to write my first book, Ozzie Smith's autobiography, *Wizard*, published in 1988. I also wrote a book on the Cardinals' 100th anniversary, in 1992. I went on to spend five years as the National League beat writer for *USA Today Baseball Weekly*, now known as *USA Today Sports Weekly*, giving me experiences that I never would have had if I had stayed in St. Louis.

My family and I moved back to St. Louis in 1996 and I had the unique opportunity to work with Buck on his autobiography, *That's A Winner*, published by Sports Publishing in 1997. It remains the favorite book that I have ever written. Writing that book convinced me that my next "job" would be writing books.

This is the 14th book that I have written about a Cardinals' player or the team itself. Even though I have maintained friendships with several of the players profiled in this book, it was fun to catch up with others who I didn't know, to find out what had happened in their lives after their days as a player ended.

The stories are varied and diverse, but I was struck by how many former Cardinals, including some who are not included in this book, have remained involved in baseball even after their playing careers were over. Every organization, it seems, has at least one former Cardinal working in some capacity. Other former players are coaching in college or high schools, or at the very least, coaching their own son's or daughter's teams in youth leagues around the country. The love of baseball they experienced as a member of the Cardinals' family is being spread elsewhere.

Fans who cheered for these players will cheer for them again as they read about what has happened in their lives post-baseball.

As happens with any family, members move away and drop out of sight. There were players I really wanted to include in this book, but they declined to be interviewed, ignored my attempts to reach them or simply could not be located. Maybe their stories can be told in a future volume, someday. But, I was lucky enough to speak with 38 former players, all of whom are included here.

Having lived in St. Louis for the better part of the last 25 years, I have learned some facts that make St. Louis, and Cardinals fans, unique. We care about where people went to high school. We enjoy toasted ravioli and frozen custard. The Rams might win the Super Bowl, but St. Louis is still, and always will be, a baseball town.

Players may get old, retire, and move away, but they are still "our guys" and part of the Cardinal Family, and we will never stop cheering for them. For that reason, I hope you enjoy catching up with these former Cardinals as much as I did.

—*Rob Rains*
January, 2005

Where Have You Gone?

CARDINALS

Where Have You Gone?

JACK CLARK

J ack Clark never wanted to leave the Cardinals.

When he became a free agent at the end of the 1987 season, he found himself right in the middle of what later was found to be collusion among the owners. It was the first step in the owners' plan to reduce players' salaries and hopefully break up the players' union.

It didn't happen, of course, but the result for Clark was that he received no offers from other teams. Even the Cardinals' offer was for a substantial cut in pay, despite his league-leading offensive numbers in 1987. When his agent, Tom Reich, mentioned the situation to his friend and combative owner of the Yankees, George Steinbrenner, Clark was soon headed for New York.

"I was a National League guy and still am," Clark said. "I was never a fan of the DH and still am not a fan of it. I like pitchers having to bat. There were a lot of things that were said to me, and the way they were said, that bothered me. I was getting a lot of pressure from the union. Tom came to me and said, 'What about the Yankees?' There was no team showing interest in any of the free agents.

"I went to New York under an assumed name and I guess other owners found out about it and the word got back to the Cardinals. The Yankees picked me up at like 5 a.m. and we went to George's office and he was there. We had already agreed to a deal and I had shaken his hand. He told me the Cardinals had called and wanted to

JACK CLARK
Seasons with Cardinals: 1985-1987

Best season with Cardinals: 1987 (All-Star; third in MVP voting)

Games: 131 • BA: .286 • **OBP: .459 (first in NL)**
SLG: .597 (first in NL) • **HR: 35 (sixth in NL)**
RBI: 106 (fourth in NL) • **R: 93** • BB: 136 (first in NL)

talk to me. A press conference was already scheduled to announce the signing. I went and called Lou Susman and he told me the Cardinals would give me the same deal the Yankees were giving me. I just felt it had come too late, and I had already given my word to George. I only talked to Susman twice, when I came to the Cardinals and when I left."

Even though Clark led the Yankees with 27 home runs in 1988, he wasn't happy. He moved on to San Diego for two seasons and completed his career with two years in Boston, retiring after the 1992 season.

He has often thought about what direction his career and life might have taken had he remained with the Cardinals.

"Looking back on it, I should have stayed a Cardinal," Clark said. "I was very happy here. I had my best years in baseball here. We went to the World Series twice in three years. It was fun to go to the ball-park every day. I was playing for the best manager in the game. My family liked it here. My kids were in school. I considered this my home."

Clark's testimony was a key reason the owners were found guilty of collusion and players like Clark received an extra shot at free agency, which allowed him to sign with the Red Sox.

The Cardinals acquired Clark in a trade from the San Francisco Giants on February 1, 1985, in an attempt to add some punch to a lineup whose top home run hitter in 1984 was David Green, with 15, and top RBI producer was George Hendrick, with 69.

It didn't take long for the love affair between Cardinals fans and Clark to bloom. He homered in his first St. Louis at bat off the Mets' Dwight Gooden and finished the 1985 campaign with 22 homers, 87 RBIs and a .281 average despite missing 36 games because of injuries.

Clark also delivered the blow that lifted the Cardinals past the Dodgers and into the World Series, a three-run homer off Tom Niedenfuer in the top of the ninth inning in Game 6 of the NLCS. In that particular at bat, Dodgers skipper Tommy Lasorda pitched to Clark with first base open instead of issuing an intentional walk.

"It was the way I had always imagined the big leagues being like," Clark said at the time. "That type of moment I had dreamed of my whole life. You hear so many stories of great players not getting there, not getting to the World Series."

Even though the Cardinals lost the Series to the Royals, they would get another chance in the postseason two years later, when they again won the pennant, this time over the Giants, and faced the Minnesota Twins in the World Series.

Unfortunately, they did it without Clark, who suffered torn ligaments in his ankle in early September. He struck out in his only pinch-hit at-bat in the NLCS, and did not play in the Series. The Twins won all four games at home to claim the world championship.

During his career, and even after he was finished playing, Clark was never the type of person who looked too far into the future. He didn't think he was going to play baseball for a living until he was drafted by the Giants in the 13th round after only two years of high school competition.

"My father was a paint maker," Clark said. "I think the most money he ever made in a year was like $13,000. He moved to California from Pennsylvania, where he had worked in the steel mills. I just grew up normal. It took me a long time to believe I was going to make it.

"I always had to learn from failure, from my mistakes. I had to teach myself. I'm just Jack, I always have been."

Since he retired as a player, Clark has been involved in numerous activities. He started a drag racing team when he was with the Padres and ran that for the first couple of years of his post-baseball life. When that experience came to an end, he took a couple of years off, riding motorcycles and spending time with his four children. He was divorced in 1998, and his former wife and children, now 24, 23, 20 and 15, all live in the Dallas area.

He decided to try to get back into baseball in 1999, and agreed to become the manager of the River City Rascals, a new independent minor league team formed in O'Fallon, Missouri, just outside St. Louis. He had a successful season and used that to land a job as a hitting coach in the Dodgers' farm system, working for Class A San Bernardino in the California League.

When changes were made to the major league team's coaching staff before the 2001 season, Clark was promoted past others in the organization and hired as the team's hitting coach. That lasted until the middle of the 2003 season when he was fired, becoming what he believes was the scapegoat for other problems on the team.

Clark spent 2004 back in the independent Frontier League, working first as the manager and then as director of baseball operations for the Columbia, Missouri, team. He also helped out former teammate Mike Henneman with a new league he was starting for junior college players in Texas.

Clark has faced personal challenges as well as his professional trials in his post-playing life. On the day before the 2003 season opener, Clark was involved in a serious motorcycle accident in Phoenix, riding from his home in Scottsdale to Bank One Ballpark for the last exhibition game against the Diamondbacks. In the summer of 2004, his father, Ralph, died after a long battle with cancer.

Clark knows he was lucky to survive his accident, which occurred as he was preparing to exit the highway. Two cars collided in another lane in front of him. The impact sent one car spinning directly in front of him. Clark attempted to get around the car, but failed. He doesn't remember anything about what happened from that point until he woke up in the hospital with a very bad headache.

"I was lucky to live," Clark said. "Somebody who came up right after the accident told police there was a man lying under a car, and I guess that was me. I had a third-degree concussion, six broken ribs, a dislocated collarbone, my hand was torn up and I had vertigo."

The 49-year-old Clark was not wearing a helmet, because Arizona law does not require it. He knows he was lucky. But that's a common theme for Clark. He still considers himself lucky with almost everything that has happened to him, during his career and after. He decided in the fall of 2004 to move from his home in Scottsdale to Augusta, Missouri, where he has purchased a home on a lake that he says makes him feel likes he's on vacation 365 days a year.

He would like to get back into baseball, either as a hitting instructor or as a minor league manager. But whatever happens, he knows that he will be busy and active.

"When I signed with the Giants I thought I would be there forever," Clark said. "When I got married and had kids, I thought that would last, but it didn't. When those things happen, it doesn't mean you throw in the towel. You keep going. It's a work in progress. You keep evolving.

"I like teaching, I like coaching. I would like to be a manager some day. Whatever happens, I am just glad to be back in the St. Louis area. The people here have always been so friendly and so respectful of me. I still like riding motorcycles out in the country. I am looking forward to living here again.

"There really is nothing that I would change about my life even if I had the chance."

Where Have You Gone?

REX HUDLER

Anytime God talks, Rex Hudler listens.

It was true on the day Hudler's wife, Jennifer, gave birth to their son Cade in 1997 and the couple knew he had been born with Down Syndrome. It was true the day he had the final at-bat of his professional career, in a minor league game, and was hit in the head by a pitch. It was true the day in 2000 that Hudler became ill and didn't know what was wrong. It turned out he was suffering from a brain hemorrhage. It was true in the summer of 2003, when Hudler was arrested at the Kansas City airport and charged with possession of marijuana.

"God is still trying to work on me, to refine me and make me better," Hudler said.

All of those moments were very traumatic times in Hudler's life and each of them individually might have been enough to bring down a weaker man. Collectively, it is amazing that Hudler is still the always positive, upbeat individual who became so popular when he played for the Cardinals from 1990-92.

"I'm happier than I've ever been in my life," Hudler says now. "God has blessed me. I don't know why He has done that, but I am very grateful."

Hudler is working as a television broadcaster for the Anaheim Angels, a job that allows him to spend quality time at home with Jennifer and their four children—Melissa, 10; Cade, seven; William,

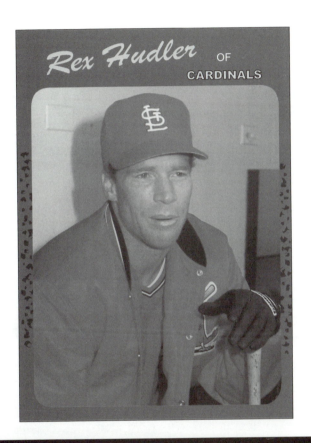

REX HUDLER
Seasons with Cardinals: 1990-1992

Best season with Cardinals: 1990

Games: 89 (as a Cardinal) • At-bats: 217 • BA: .281 • OBP: .323
SLG: .447 • HR: 7 • RBI: 22 • R: 30 • SB: 18

three; and David, who will be two in 2005. The couple has been very active in raising money for Down's Syndrome, starting a charity, Team Up for Down Syndrome, when Hudler was with the Philadelphia Phillies. Today, they continue the event in southern California.

Hudler will be the first person to tell you that he did not have as much raw physical ability as many players, but he got the most out of what he did have. Because he was a first-round pick by the Yankees in the 1978 draft, the 18th overall selection, many people viewed his 14-year career as a disappointment.

That group would not include Hudler or Cardinals fans, who quickly adopted him as one of their favorites when the Cardinals acquired him from Montreal in April 1990 for reliever John Costello.

His aggressive style, his determination to go all out on every play, was what drew fans to Hudler. He admitted that he sometimes tried to stretch a double into a triple, even though he knew he might get thrown out, so that he could make a head-first dive into the base and get the crowd riled up.

Hudler stayed with the Cardinals through the 1992 season, and his best year was his first, 1990. He played in just 89 games, but appeared at every position except pitcher or catcher. He hit .281 with 11 doubles, two triples, seven homers, 22 RBIs and 18 stolen bases.

He even had his likeness immortalized on a t-shirt, drawn by artist and teammate Bob Tewksbury.

The Cardinals released Hudler after the 1992 season so that he could sign a lucrative offer to play in Japan for a year. He then completed his major-league career in 1998 after three seasons with the Angels and finally a year-plus in Philadelphia.

After retiring early in the 1998 season, Hudler decided later that summer that he still did not have baseball out of his system. So, he signed a Triple A contract with Cleveland. He knew he was nearing the end of a 21-year career, including 10 years in the majors, but he couldn't decide how he wanted his career to end. Hudler thinks God took care of that for him.

"I asked the manager if I could play one more game, at second base. He said sure." Hudler recalls. "My first at-bat I struck out. The second time up I got a routine hit, but I rounded first and kept running. I slid under the tag, but the umpire called me out. I had a nice strawberry on my knee and blood on my arm.

"I had never been hit in the head in my career, and my third time up, I got hit right in the back of the neck. I heard God's voice louder than ever before: 'I told you to leave last night.' That was my last at-bat. God was telling me He had something else planned for me."

Hudler had no idea what that would be, even though he was interested in broadcasting and had done some postseason work during the later years of his playing career. Still, he was not prepared when his phone rang a couple of days later. It was the Angels, who wanted to hire him as one of their broadcasters.

He was working for the Angels when he started complaining of a headache on a flight from Texas to Oakland in 2000. When he got to his hotel room he became nauseous and threw up. He called Jennifer, who told him to call the front desk for help. Two minutes later, paramedics were in his room.

As they wheeled him down to a waiting ambulance, Hudler saw a boy with Down Syndrome. "He told me I was going to be fine," Hudler said. "I know he was God's messenger.

"I didn't feel threatened at the time, because I didn't realize it was life threatening. I still had my cell phone, and somehow it called my wife, so she was able to hear the conversation in the ambulance and knew what was happening. She flew to Oakland and after I got to the hospital they said I had a brain hemorrhage.

"I had a silver dollar-sized blood spot on the back of my brain. Jennifer had them move me to Stanford, one of the best hospitals in the country, while the doctors decided what to do. Before they had made up their mind, the spot disappeared and the bleeding stopped. Nobody knew why. On the second day the pain went away and on the third day the spot was gone.

"The best neurosurgeons in the country didn't understand it, but I knew why—God had healed me."

Hudler also understands now why he was arrested in the Kansas City airport in the summer of 2003 as the Angels were leaving town. The airport screener pulled a small box out of his luggage, and a police officer pulled out a pipe and banged it hard on a table, knocking out bits of marijuana residue.

He was handcuffed and taken to jail, where he spent a couple of hours. When the arrest became public, he was suspended from his job with the Angels for the rest of the year. He had to deal with letters and comments from fans who felt he had betrayed them, and he stood up and faced them and listened to what they had to say.

Because the amount of marijuana involved was very small, the charges were quickly dropped after Hudler agreed to perform community service and to receive treatment.

Still, his image was affected, and nobody knew that better than Hudler. He understood that it was another message from God, providing him with yet another platform to speak of his problems of the past.

Hudler later admitted he had smoked marijuana off and on since he was a senior in high school.

"It made me feel good, it relaxed me," he told the *Los Angeles Times*. "It was easy, there was no real side effect. I knew it was wrong, but I liked it."

After missing the rest of the season, Hudler was reinstated by the Angels in November 2003.

"It was one of the worst times of my life," Hudler said of his arrest and suspension. "But it was soul-searching, and I am grateful for it now because it made me a better person.

"We all make mistakes, but it seems I have to learn the hard way. I was just grateful the Angels realized I am an upbeat, positive, fun, inspirational guy who made a mistake. Luckily they cut me some slack.

"I thought I might lose my job, but I knew if that happened God would take us in another direction."

Hudler still considers the three years he spent with the Cardinals the best years of his playing career. Mike Shannon gave him the nickname "Hurricane," and others started calling him "Wonderdog." The fans loved his enthusiasm and his attitude, and he loved the crowd.

"I fed off the crowd," he said. "It was fun for me. I loved entertaining the crowd. It's what I miss the most. It was a great time in my life."

Hudler has never been the type of person who dwells in the past or looks backward, however. He is always looking ahead, wondering what his next challenge is going to be.

He just hopes he has received all of the serious messages from God that he needs to hear for a while.

DAL MAXVILL

Dal Maxvill has the Cardinals to thank for allowing him to lead the perfect retiree lifestyle—travel extensively, live through the cold winter months in Florida and spend the rest of the year relaxing with his family.

It wasn't his 13-year playing career that gave him the freedom to spend his "golden years" in such a manner, however, it was the 10 years he spent as the team's general manager, from 1985 to 1995.

Maxvill was the shocking choice of the Cardinals to take over as general manager, a decision that was surprising even to him. He was working as the third base coach of the Atlanta Braves, and also was the co-owner of Cardinal Travel. He and teammate Joe Hoerner had gone into the travel business in 1969, and he was at Busch Stadium making a pitch to Bing Devine about starting a booster club for the Cardinals.

Lou Susman, an attorney for Gussie Busch, sent word that he wanted to talk to Maxvill, and Maxvill agreed to meet with him. Susman said he was trying to get input about the organization and it wasn't until about two hours into their meeting that Maxvill realized he was being interviewed for the GM job. Several more interviews followed before Maxvill finally was offered and accepted the job.

During his first five years as GM, the Cardinals went to the World Series twice and were in the pennant race again in September 1989 when injuries to Todd Worrell and Willie McGee knocked them out

DAL MAXVILL
Seasons with Cardinals as a general manager: 1985-1995
Seasons with Cardinals as a player: 1962-1972

Best season with Cardinals: 1968 (Gold Glove)

Games: 151 • At-bats: 459 • BA: .253 • HR: 1 • RBI: 24 • R: 51

of the race. As the home-grown players on those teams aged and became free agents, however, Maxvill and the Cardinals struggled to replace them. As a result, the last five years of his tenure were not nearly as enjoyable as the first five.

"Probably my biggest disappointment was that I couldn't convince the powers that be that we needed more of an investment into the ballclub other than just the farm system," Maxvill said. "We needed to replace the free agents who were leaving us and I could never convince August (Busch) that the ballclub needed to dip into their savings account (the brewery) so we could sign a major free agent.

"He was not into that at all. There were no excuses, but it was disappointing. I understood August had to report to the stockholders and he didn't want to report that we were spending $30 million on a free agent pitcher. He didn't think that money was ever going to come back."

Maxvill was convinced that pitcher Greg Maddux, for one, would have signed with the Cardinals instead of the Atlanta Braves if the team had been able to make him a competitive offer.

"Many players had a strong interest in coming to St. Louis, but we couldn't make them an offer," Maxvill said.

Joe Torre was Maxvill's manager during those latter years. After Torre was fired in St. Louis by new general manager Walt Jocketty and moved on to manage the Yankees, Maxvill called Torre on the phone with a question.

"I asked him if it was more fun to try to be competitive with a $27 million club like we had, or with a team like the Yankees, whose payroll had to be about $70 million even then," Maxvill said. "He gave me the answer I expected—that it was a challenge with the $27 million payroll, but it was a whole lot more fun with the $70 million team."

Maxvill spent the bulk of his playing career with the Cardinals. He made his major-league debut in 1962 and saw limited duty during his first two seasons. In 1964, he was optioned back to the minor leagues during the middle of the year. A graduate of Washington University with an engineering degree, Maxvill had a standing job offer when he was ready to leave baseball. He considered it but instead was talked into reporting to the minor leagues.

The decision paid off when Maxvill was recalled later in the season and was awarded the starting spot at second base in all seven games of the '64 World Series. Filling in for the injured Julian Javier, Maxvill caught the final out to clinch the world championship.

Maxvill took over as the starting shortstop in 1965, replacing Dick Groat, remained there through two more pennant-winning years, in 1967 and 1968, up through the 1972 season, when he was traded to Oakland. He was never much of an offensive threat, but played well defensively and was a key player on those championship clubs. His best season average was .253 in 1968, and he hit only six career homers, all with the Cardinals. However, one of them was significant—the first grand slam hit outside the United States, at Jarry Park in Montreal.

Maxvill appeared in another World Series for the A's in 1974, before his playing career ended after 13 years in 1975 after shuffling back and forth from the A's to the Pirates.

Maxvill is still a fan of the Cardinals and Yankees. He has not worked in baseball since doing some spring training scouting for the Yankees in 1996 and 1997 after leaving the Cardinals.

He does miss the game, however.

"I miss being around the baseball people," Maxvill said. "I miss the scouts and the personnel people, the minor league folks, some of the media. I miss the connection to the game, and I miss the money."

Maxvill doesn't miss the agents, the media scrutiny under which he constantly worked or his frustrating experiences dealing with the beancounters at Anheuser-Busch.

When Maxvill retired after the 1975 season, he didn't have any major post-baseball plans. He worked some at the travel agency, but decided he was better off as the co-owner than as a day-to-day worker. He became the sole owner in 1996 when Hoerner was killed in a tractor accident. Maxvill's sister has run the business the past 25 years, but is planning on retiring in 2005, making the future of the business uncertain.

"I never had any other enterprises," Maxvill said. "I didn't open a tavern or a restaurant. I wish I had opened a filling station with gas costing $2 a gallon. I really just hoped to stay in baseball as long as I could, and I stayed for quite a while."

Indeed he did—30-plus years. Following his playing career Maxvill coached with the Mets and Cardinals, worked as a minor-league infield instructor for the Cardinals and as a coach for Torre in Atlanta before becoming the Cardinals' general manager.

"I thought I knew what the job would be, that the general manager basically ran the ballclub and oversaw the operations of the farm system and scouting departments," he said. "I had no idea about the time demands of the job itself and dealing with the media. It was a lot greater than I expected. I just hoped to do a good job and hang around a while, and I was lucky enough to last for 10 years."

Asked if he had any desire to be a general manager in the current baseball environment, Maxvill had a quick answer: no.

He would rather spend his time doing precisely what he is doing now, traveling with his wife Diane to Europe or South America, or spending time at their condo in St. Petersburg, Florida. They have four children and six grandchildren, with a seventh due in 2005, all of whom live in the St. Louis area.

"Hopefully we will keep doing what we are doing for the next several years," said Maxvill, who will be 66 in 2005. "It's a good life. We are very fortunate that our kids are all healthy, and fortunate to have been involved in the game of baseball."

JOHN MORRIS

John Morris has no problems recalling the best day of his baseball career.

It was a Sunday, September 20, 1987, and the first-place Cardinals were playing the Cubs at Busch Stadium. Morris had missed three days while attending his father's funeral in New York. When he walked into the clubhouse that morning, coach Dave Ricketts told him, "Whitey wants to see you."

Morris thought manager Whitey Herzog likely was just going to offer his condolences, welcome him back and tell him to be ready to pinch-hit by the seventh inning, his normal role on the team that season.

Instead, when Morris walked into Herzog's office, the manager held up two lineup cards for that day's game, one with Morris starting and playing right field, batting seventh, the other with him on the bench.

"What do you want to do kid," Herzog asked. "I'm leaving it up to you."

It took Morris a moment to say, "I guess I want to play," to which Herzog responded, "go get some hits for your dad."

That's exactly what Morris did. He drove in two runs with a single in the second inning, drove in another run with a groundout in the third and singled in another run with the bases loaded in the fifth as the Cardinals beat Greg Maddux and the Cubs 10-2.

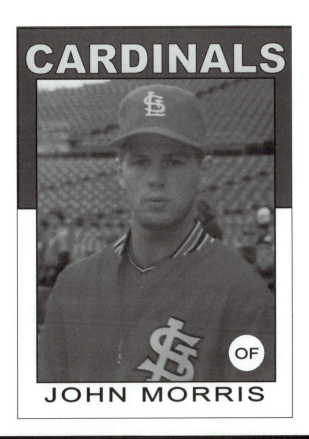

JOHN MORRIS
Seasons with Cardinals: 1986-1990

Best season with Cardinals: 1987

Games: 101 • At bats: 157 • BA: .261 • HR: 3 • RBI: 23 • R: 22

The four RBIs were a career high for Morris, who also received a standing ovation from the nearly 50,000 fans in attendance at Busch following his last hit. Morris had just 23 RBIs that season and 63 RBIs in his major-league career.

"I realize that Whitey was challenging me," Morris said. "He had so many other options to play right field that day. I hadn't played in four days. Everybody in the park knew what was going on. I remember standing on first thinking to myself, 'This is the greatest baseball city in the world.'"

Morris, a former number-one pick of the Kansas City Royals in 1982 who was traded to the Cardinals in 1985 for Lonnie Smith, learned a lot about baseball, and the psychology of the sport, during his seven years in the majors with the Cardinals, Phillies and Angels. Since retiring after the 1992 season, he has tried to use the knowledge he has gained as a coach in the minor leagues.

He will be coaching in the Phillies' system for the sixth season in 2005, probably returning to Double A Reading, Pennsylvania. He also has managed for one season at Class A Clearwater and missed the 2003 season after undergoing back fusion surgery which left him in a full body cast for 10 weeks. He moved to Reading when he was divorced two years ago after living for 15 years in Florida.

Morris, who completed his college degree at Seton Hall, has begun spending more of his time working with players off the field as well as on.

"After 10 years of [coaching] I finally realized that most of the problems players have have nothing to do with what is going on on the field," Morris said. "Something is usually getting in the way. Why can't a guy hit better? Why does he keep getting picked off? Why can't he hit the cutoff man? The player's focus is so off because they are distracted by other things going on in their lives.

"I want to take coaching to the next step. Usually we [coaches] become obsessed that if we fix one thing, like where a batter holds his hands on the bat, everything will be okay. I want to help athletes reach their potential, and I know there is more involved than that."

Morris, who will turn 44 in 2005, has been undergoing "coaching" himself from professionals.

"I want to know what the things are that stop me, what gets in my way of being as effective as I can possibly be," Morris said. "Somewhere down the line I can really see myself doing this full time."

Morris was never a full-time player during his career, but he said he has no regrets. He especially enjoyed his years in St. Louis, where he became most famous for his impersonations of teammate Willie McGee. The two remain good friends, and McGee wrote the foreword for a book written by Morris, *Bullet Bob Comes to Louisville*, published by Diamond Communications in 1999.

Morris said the impersonations became famous in spring training of 1989.

"I was just hanging out one day with only a few days left in Florida and Whitey said, 'Hey, before the game tomorrow I want you to do your McGee impersonation to get the crowd going.' I got a lot of the players involved and we did an entire skit. I impersonated Willie batting, then I got on base and got picked off. I looked in the dugout and he was on the floor because he was laughing so hard.

"Bob Costas was at the game and saw it, and NBC was still doing the Game of the Week then. He came up to me after the game and said if I could do the entire skit again the next day, they would film it and run it on the pregame show. We did, and it was hilarious. Whitey told me my job on the team was to keep Willie laughing."

There were a lot of laughs on the Cardinals' teams in the mid-1980s.

"We were in Pittsburgh one time and Danny Cox went into this gag shop and bought a bag of rubber potato chips," Morris said. "He took them to the clubhouse and dumped the whole bag into a bowl of regular chips and mixed them all together.

"Some guys were sitting there playing cards, and Whitey walked up behind them and reached in to grab a handful of chips. He got one of the rubber ones, and threw it back in the bowl. 'Those things are [expletive]' he said and walked away. Those were some special times."

Where Have You Gone?

KEN REITZ

K en Reitz is still spending his days trying to hit a little white ball these days, but this ball is sitting on a tee instead of being thrown 90 miles an hour.

He is not sure which is harder or which is more enjoyable.

"It ranks right up there," Reitz said of golf.

Reitz had two stays with the Cardinals during his major league career, which lasted from 1972 to 1982, and still maintains his home in the St. Louis suburb of St. Charles. In addition to his pursuit of golf, he does frequent public appearances and clinics on behalf of the Cardinals.

His biggest passion is golf, however, and for the past eight years he has been a regular member of the Celebrity Players Tour, a group of former professional athletes and other celebrities who have taken their love for competition onto the golf course.

Reitz said he fooled around a little with golf as a youngster growing up but did not become hooked on the game until he retired from baseball. He was living in the country near a nine-hole course, and started to play when asked by a friend.

"We would bet $5 or $10 and it was a fun time," Reitz said. "I liked the game, and it kind of grew. I was invited to a celebrity tournament in Toronto and finished 10th, and then I really started to get into it."

ST. LOUIS CARDINALS

KEN
REITZ   3rd BASE

KEN REITZ
Seasons with Cardinals: 1972-1975; 1977-1980

Best season with Cardinals: 1977

Games: 157 • BA: .261 • 2B: 36 (seventh in NL)
HR: 17 • RBI: 79 • R: 58

When he is not playing one of the dozen or so celebrity tournaments during the year in the United States, Canada and Jamaica, Reitz can be found nearly every day at Bogey Hills Country Club, where he lives in a condo on the golf course.

"We have a group that comes out almost every day from Tuesday through Sunday." Reitz said. "As long as it isn't sleeting or snowing we will be out there."

Reitz finally experienced the joy of success in golf that he had experienced in baseball in the summer of 2004, when after 10 years of trying, he won his first tournament on the tour, in Dayton, Ohio.

"Winning that tournament ranks up there with anything I ever did in baseball," Reitz said. "There are always 60-70 people out there competing, and they are all really good golfers, except Charles Barkley. He is just there for fun.

"I would put winning that tournament up there with hitting my first home run in the majors, with winning a Gold Glove and with playing in the All-Star game. I was on a pretty emotional high for a couple of days."

Reitz was proud of the fact he beat the two established stars of the tour, former pitcher Rick Rhoden and former hockey star Dan Quinn, who seem to trade off winning almost all of the events.

"I shot nine under for the two days," Reitz said. "I just had two really good days where nothing went wrong."

Reitz kind of fell into his golfing career by accident. He didn't know what he would do when he retired from baseball, although he hoped to land a job somewhere in the game.

"I sent out resumes to every team and didn't come up with anything," he said. "I didn't really know what I was going to do. I was living in Franklin County, Missouri, and worked for several years there in community services. I worked with people who were in trouble for alcoholism, or writing bad checks or for other reasons. I enjoyed it okay, but it wasn't really what I wanted to do the rest of my life."

When he was 45 years old, Reitz was able to begin drawing his baseball pension, and that coincided with his rise on the celebrity tour and making more appearances for the Cardinals.

"I do the caravan in January and the legends camp in Florida in February, and go speak to groups with some of the sales people," he said. "When they have groups come to the ballpark I will go down there and sign autographs. I probably do about 20 or 25 things a year for them."

He also is around the ballpark a lot even when he is not working, as he has remained a fan of the game. He thinks he even appreciates the game more now since he has stopped playing than he did as a player.

"You can watch and appreciate the skills of the players," Reitz said. "I do think the game has changed. The parks are smaller, and I don't think the pitching is as dominant. Teams don't go into a city and face three quality starters every series like we did when I played."

Reitz was nicknamed "The Zamboni" for his defensive excellence at third base. He won only one Gold Glove, in 1975, but likely could have earned several more if he had not had the misfortune of playing the same position at the same time as the Phillies' Mike Schmidt, who dominated the voting.

It was actually an error that he was charged that which marked one of Reitz's best known days in a Cardinal uniform. Pitcher Bob Forsch recorded his first no-hitter in 1978 when a ball many observers believed should have been called a hit was instead ruled as an error on Reitz.

"The Zamboni" has been out of commission as of late after undergoing a second rotator cuff operation in November 2004. Reitz says that aside from the surgery, he feels better today than he did when he was playing baseball 25 years ago.

"In the later part of my career, baseball became such a grind," Reitz said. "It really wears you down and makes you feel older than you are."

Another factor in the difference in Reitz's health was that he became hooked on amphetamines while he was playing for the Cubs in 1981, after he was traded to Chicago along with Leon Durham as part of the Bruce Sutter deal.

"Probably the biggest thing I would look back on and change about my career is when I got to Chicago I started taking amphetamines," Reitz said. "That probably took four years off my career and caused a lot of problems."

Reitz said the addiction started innocently enough, as it often does.

"Somebody gave them to me one day and it helped," Reitz said. "I said, 'Hey those make me feel pretty good,' and it just went from there. They didn't have the same level of education about drugs back then as they have today. Today the players know more and they take better care of themselves. That was the only bad habit I had."

Reitz has a son who recently graduated from Southeast Missouri State, and a daughter in California who recently gave birth to her first child, making Reitz a grandfather for the first time. That allows him to fit right in with the other retired grandpas he competes with every day on the golf course, either at Bogey Hills or on the celebrity tour.

"I live a pretty modest life, but to me it's a pretty perfect world," Reitz said.

Where Have You Gone?

DANNY COX

Living in the middle of 788 acres near Freeburg, Illinois, 30 miles east of St. Louis, Danny Cox and his family don't have many neighbors. He can look out his back windows and see a 21-acre lake—not other people's back yards. He sees a lot more deer, turkeys, raccoons, coyotes, fox, possum, ducks and geese than he does people.

"I always wanted to have some land and live out in the country," Cox said. "I always tell people that you can go visit the city, but you can't always visit the country."

The son of a military officer, Cox moved often when he was a youngster. So when he got the chance to settle down and fulfill his dream of living in the country, he seized the opportunity. He bought the old strip mining land in 1987, put in roads and built the house where he has been living since 1988.

"The family enjoys it," Cox said. "Even though we don't have many neighbors, a lot of people come out to go hunting or fishing."

Cox might be adding some neighbors in the near future, though. He is considering a plan to take some of his land on one edge of his property, perhaps as much as 150 to 200 acres, and build a housing development which would also feature horseback riding trails, a stable and an indoor arena.

"It would be kind of like the developments that are built around golf courses, but instead of people going golfing they would be going

Focus on Sport/Getty Images

DANNY COX
Seasons with Cardinals: 1983-1988

Best season with Cardinals: 1985

Games: 35 (eighth in NL) • Record: 18-9 (sixth in NL in wins)
ERA: 2.88 (eighth in NL) • IP: 241 (ninth in NL) • Hits: 226
SO: 131 • CG: 10 (fourth in NL) • SHO: 4 (fifth in NL)

horseback riding," Cox said. "My wife and daughter ride and they really enjoy it. I jump on a horse every now and then."

There are two lakes in this area of the property, one five acres and the other seven acres, and Cox envisions building the homes around those lakes.

"A lot of people enjoy riding horses but have no place to go," Cox said. "Here you just go out in your backyard, jump on your horse and take off."

A 13th-round draft choice of the Cardinals in 1981, Cox made it to the major leagues just two years later. He pitched for St. Louis through the 1988 season, then missed the next two years because of injuries.

Cox returned to the majors in 1991 with the Phillies, where he remained in 1992. He finished his career with three years in Toronto, where he finally won a World Series ring in 1993, winning seven games and saving two for the Blue Jays' second straight championship team.

His best season came in the pennant-winning year of 1985, when he went 18-9 with a 2.88 ERA. Even though his ERA was almost exactly the same the following year, 2.90, his record slipped to 12-13. In 1987, another pennant-winning season, he was 11-9 with a 3.88 ERA. Cox provided Cardinals fans with their greatest memory of his days in St. Louis during the postseason that year. His clutch, eight-hit shutout of the San Francisco Giants in Game 7 of the National League Championship Series lifted the Cardinals to their third pennant in six seasons and a trip to the World Series, where they eventually lost in seven games to the Minnesota Twins.

Cox won 74 games in his major-league career.

Hunting, fishing and working on his plans for the horseback riding development is not all that has kept Cox busy since he retired as a player after the 1995 season. He and his wife, Nancy, are the parents of three children—sons Kyle, 14, and Kamden, nine, and daughter Kayleigh, 12—which keep him busy. He also has spent the past four seasons coaching and managing the Gateway Grizzles, an independent minor league team in the Frontier League, which plays in nearby Sauget, Illinois.

After working as the team's pitching coach for its first two seasons, Cox took over as the manager in 2003 and led the team to the Frontier League championship. The Grizzlies lost in the playoffs in 2004, but Cox is hoping the team can reclaim its title in 2005.

"Managing in independent baseball is different than working in an organization, because we have control of the players," Cox said. "If somebody isn't working out we can go out and get somebody else. We don't have to play a guy because somebody sitting behind a desk somewhere thinks he is a prospect."

Cox has enjoyed the challenge and still enjoys putting a uniform on every day during the summer. "It's just a little larger uniform now," he said. "It's what I know, it's what I'm used to."

Cox was a little disappointed that he was not considered for the job of managing the Cardinals' Double A farm team that moved to Springfield, Missouri, for the 2005 season. His goal is to make it back to the major leagues someday as a manager or pitching coach, but he knows that likely will not happen until he gets back to working within a major league organization.

He does not want to make the sacrifices he would have to make with his personal life, however, to manage a Class A team in Florida, California, or some other far-off state.

"I was interested in the Springfield job because it was a step up in league, it was close by and it was a Cardinals team," Cox said. "I was hoping it would work out."

Since that didn't happen, however, Cox will return to the Grizzlies, a job he definitely enjoys.

"I like the responsibility of being in charge of all the players," Cox said. "When you are playing you are basically selfish, because the only person you are worried about is yourself. I like the aspect of running the team and being in charge of everybody."

GREG MATHEWS

Greg Mathews did not really learn the power of baseball until years after his major-league career came to an end.

He had not planned on having his career end when he was 30 years old. But after failing to fully recover from a torn ligament in his left elbow, that's what happened. He spent several years struggling to find a purpose in his post-baseball life—other than to feel depressed and upset that his career had come to a premature end.

The purpose came when he began to put on clinics and camps for kids, with a portion of the proceeds being donated to the Ranken-Jordan pediatric rehabilitation center in St. Louis.

"I just fell in love with the program," Mathews said. "A lot of these kids feel like they got a raw deal, and I could relate. What I went through was so difficult, even if it was far different circumstances."

That exposure to Ranken-Jordan led Mathews to go to work full-time for the center, where he is now vice president of marketing and development.

He uses baseball as part of the therapy the children receive at the center. Patients there range in age from two weeks old to 18 years old; their ailments may range from injuries suffered in a car accident to a serious illness or other trauma. The average length of each child's stay at the center is 30 days.

"We help them make the transition after the hospital gets them well," Mathews said. "We continue the therapy. We help them improve mentally, socially and emotionally."

GREG MATHEWS
Seasons with Cardinals: 1986-1990

Best season with Cardinals: 1987

Games: 32 • Record: 11-11 • ERA: 3.73 • IP: 197.7
Hits: 184 • SO: 101 • CG: 2 • SHO: 1

Mathews often throws batting practice to kids still in a wheelchair. He never will forget one such episode.

"The boy was on the verge of trying to walk but he had no incentive," Mathews said. "Baseball was his incentive to get him to walk. He got braces and got out of the chair because he wanted to stand up and hit the baseball. Other kids saw that and that gave them the same incentive."

When he isn't working with the kids, Mathews's job is to help raise money so the center can continue its work. Ranken-Jordan is in the midst of a $26 million fundraising campaign and needs to raise $1.7 million by the end of June 2005 to meet its goal.

"For years the center was funded by an endowment from Mary Ranken, but that money is running out," Mathews said. "My job is to help raise the awareness of the need to support Ranken-Jordan. Any child could become a patient here at any time. That's something a lot of people don't want to think about, but it's true."

When he was pitching for the Cardinals, Mathews never envisioned himself becoming involved in this kind of work. He won 11 games as a rookie in 1986, repeated that success the next year and found himself starting the fourth game of the World Series against the Twins, receiving a no-decision.

He didn't know that he was only months away from injuring his elbow, and that he would win only six more games over the next five years in his major-league career.

Mathews sat out all of the 1989 season, was 0-5 for the Cardinals in 1990, became a free agent, was signed and released by the Royals and Brewers in 1991, then signed with the Phillies and was 2-3 there in 1992 before his career came to an end.

"My college degree is in exercise psychology and I have a master's in media communications, so I really thought I would be a coach or an announcer," Mathews said.

Neither of those careers ever came about. One of his first postbaseball businesses was to open a center that offered pitching and hitting lessons to youngsters, but Mathews quickly tired of that experience.

"I realized that 99 percent of the kids we were working with were not going to make it, and that was very disheartening to me," Mathews said. "These kids truly had the passion for the game, but they were not good enough that they were ever going to make it."

It was working in that business, however, which led Mathews to Ranken-Jordan.

"I never imagined that I would be helping kids with special needs using baseball as a medium," Mathews said. "The best thing about it is you can see the positives, you can see the kids improving. These kids have been through difficult times and they need guidance. I talk to them about my career and my experiences. As much as I am helping these kids, they have helped me.

"I have realized that I need to focus on the things that I can do, not the things I can't do, and that's the same as these kids. I feel fortunate that I am able to do what I do. I don't spend any more time thinking about what I might have done in baseball had I not been injured. I appreciate baseball and what it is doing for these kids more now than I ever did when I was playing."

Even a simple game of catch, which millions of youngsters take for granted, can be something special with these kids, Mathews said.

"It gives them positive reinforcement," he said. "They have to focus on doing one thing, catching the ball. Then they focus on throwing it. It really helps develop their hand-eye coordination. They see that other kids are going through exactly the same thing they are going through."

Mathews, a divorced father of three children—aged 19, 16 and 11—takes the situation of each one of the patients very personally because he knows in most cases, they are at Ranken-Jordan because they became the victim of something that was not their fault.

"We had a 17-year-old boy in here whose family moved from Colorado to East St. Louis," Mathews said. "He was wearing the wrong jacket one day and somebody in a gang shot him. Now he's paralyzed. That was not his fault. He didn't know he was wearing the jacket of a rival gang.

"Our goal with him is to help build his self-esteem and to realize that this happened for a reason. He has to make the best of his life. His life is just beginning."

Those are the lessons that Mathews tries to teach every day.

"I could have a pity party because my career didn't work out like I wanted, but what good would that do?" he said. "I'm utilizing other talents. Every time I walk in here I feel so fortunate to be here."

TOM NIETO

Tom Nieto had a pretty short window to decide if he wanted to stay in baseball after the end of his playing career.

"I went to spring training with Cincinnati in 1992 and I lasted about three weeks before I realized my shoulder just wouldn't let me play anymore," Nieto said. "I was wasting my time and their time.

"Jim Bowden was the GM and he offered me a minor league coaching job right away. He told me 'Just take your stuff and put it in the coaches' room' and that's what I did."

Thirteen years later, Nieto is still working in baseball, beginning the 2005 season as a major league coach with the New York Mets. He will be one of the few coaches hired specifically to work with catchers at the major league level.

"Outfielders have coaches to hit them fly balls and infielders get ground balls before every game, but nobody works with the catchers," Nieto said. "That's what they hired me to do."

Nieto has coached and managed in the minors for the Reds, Yankees and Cardinals, even spending two years as a major league coach with the Yankees under Joe Torre. That was where he became friends with Willie Randolph, the new manager of the Mets, who hired him for his staff.

When Bowden offered Nieto the job and he agreed to become a coach with Double-A Chattanooga, he really had no idea if he would like the job and accompanying lifestyle or not. As it turned out, he

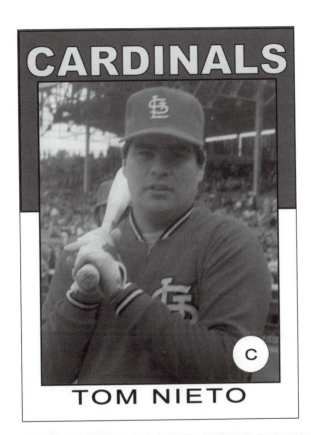

CARDINALS

TOM NIETO

C

TOM NIETO
Seasons with Cardinals: 1984-1985

Best season with Cardinals: 1985

Games: 95 • At-bats: 253 • BA: .225 • RBI: 34 • OBP: .305

enjoyed it very much and decided staying in baseball beat the alternative of going back home to southern California and working in the family construction business.

"I had gone to Pittsburgh in 1991 and realized that I couldn't play anymore, so I went back home," Nieto said. "I spent the summer learning the ins and outs of the construction business. My brother and my cousin work there, my father worked there, and my uncle runs it. By the end of that summer I decided baseball was a hell of a job.

"I take my hat off to my dad and brother and the rest of the family that works there. They've been doing it for so long, and it really is a demanding job. They are out there busting their rump for 40 hours or more a week."

Nieto found his excuse to leave when Ted Simmons, then the Cardinals' farm director, called and offered him a chance to join the Triple A team in Memphis.

"He said they needed a catcher for the last month of the season, and I agreed to do it," Nieto said. "I joined the team in Des Moines and thought I would have a week or so to get in shape. I hadn't touched a baseball for three months. But the first day I got there, I was in there."

Nieto enjoyed the final month, and that was what gave him the incentive to try to play one more year the following spring with Cincinnati, which gave him the opening he needed to begin his coaching career.

"The first couple of years I managed I really got the bug to do it," he said. "I really enjoyed the Xs and Os, the strategy of the game. Once I got into it I was really hooked."

Nieto said he really had not expected to stay involved with the game after he was finished playing, or else he would have paid more attention to that side of the game during his career. As a catcher, he was more involved than many of the players, but he knows he could have learned more from Whitey Herzog and the other managers he played for.

Nieto was the Cardinals' backup catcher in 1984 and 1985. His major career highlight, like most fortunate players, came when he was able to play in the 1985 World Series. A third-round pick by the

Cardinals in the 1981 draft, Nieto made his major league debut by catching 33 games in 1984, posting a .279 average with three homers and 12 RBIs. He caught 95 games in 1985 but was not much of an offensive threat, hitting just .225 with no homers and 34 RBIs. He caught two games in the World Series against the Royals, going 0 for 5.

He was traded to Montreal at the end of spring training in 1986 for backup infielder Fred Manrique, then moved on to Minnesota in 1987 and 1988 before playing his last regular-season games in the majors with the Phillies in 1989 and 1990.

"My son is 14 now and I tell him I have worn a uniform in the summer every year of my life since I was seven years old," Nieto said.

Once he made the decision to remain in coaching and managing, Nieto and his family moved from California to the Tampa, Florida, area. In addition to his son, Nieto and his wife, Karen, have an 18-year-old daughter who will be graduating from high school in 2005.

All of Nieto's career managing experience has been at the Class A level, four years in the Florida State League and four years in the South Atlantic League. It would be natural for him to express a desire to one day manage in the major leagues, but he is content to not think about that yet.

"I'm only 44 and I probably would have some more managing to do, at a higher level in the minors, before that would be a possibility," Nieto said. "I'm very happy doing what I'm doing."

Nieto just hopes his current major league assignment doesn't end the way his last stint in the big leagues did.

"I was with the Yankees for two years, working with the catchers, but when we lost to the Angels in the first round of the playoffs in 2002 (George) Steinbrenner fired me," Nieto said. "I guess I was the reason we lost."

RAY WASHBURN

During the 12 years he worked as a college baseball coach, Ray Washburn stressed two important fundamentals to his players—develop proper mechanics, and make certain you earn your college degree.

Washburn knows that even though he made it to the major leagues and spent nine of his 10 years there pitching for the Cardinals, he would have been lost for the rest of his life if he had not been able to get his college degree, which led to his being hired as the baseball coach and later the athletics director, for 11 years, at Bellevue Community College in his native Washington state.

He also knows that the great majority of his college players will never make it to the major leagues or even sign a professional contract, making that college degree all the more important.

"When I got out of baseball I needed about eight hours to finish my degree and when I got that completed, I had the opportunity to take the coaching job," Washburn said. "While I was coaching I even had the opportunity to go back to school and earn my master's degree, and I was glad I did that."

Only two of his players that he coached at Bellevue made it to the major leagues, including former Cardinal pitcher Kevin Hagen.

"My biggest message to them is to go to school and make good grades because then you will have the opportunity to go somewhere (beyond junior college)," Washburn said. "You might get the chance

RAY WASHBURN
Seasons with Cardinals: 1961-1969

Best season with Cardinals: 1968

Games: 31 • Record: 14-8 • **ERA: 2.26 (eighth in NL)** • IP: 215
Hits: 191 • SO: 124 • **CG: 8** • SHO: 4

to continue to play while you are getting an education. They need to realize how important that is going to be for them. They have to have the education to fall back on if a baseball career doesn't work out."

Washburn said he never had any great teams during his coaching days, but that his squads were always very competitive in a good junior college conference that included schools in Washington and Oregon.

Washburn, who will be 67 in 2005, is now retired from full-time work at the college but stays active by teaching a couple of activity classes each semester.

"It gives me something to do in the winters, and I enjoy the students," he said. "I enjoy the atmosphere. I really don't think college students have changed all that much over the years. They are still very enthusiastic, and working with them helps keep me younger, too."

When Washburn isn't teaching, he enjoys spending time with his wife, Bev, and their three children and five grandchildren. One of his sons is living in Germany, working as an architect, but the others are all within a couple of hours' drive from their home, he said.

One of his sons-in-law is involved in the orchard business, and Washburn helps him during the busy season by picking the trees and doing the other jobs that need to be done.

"It's very peaceful out there in the middle of an orchard," he said. "There's nobody to bother you."

Washburn pitched for the Cardinals from 1961 through 1969, although he was injured for much of the first part of his career, spending almost three years recovering from a torn triceps muscle. The best season of his career was 1968, when he was 14-8 with a 2.26 ERA and also pitched the first no-hitter by a Cardinal in 27 years.

It came at Candlestick Park in San Francisco, two days after the Cardinals had clinched the pennant, and the day after Gaylord Perry had no-hit the Cardinals. Washburn was not even aware of Perry's no-hitter until the following morning because he had left the ballpark early to prepare for his afternoon start the following day.

Washburn allowed just two fly balls in the game and completed the game by retiring Hall of Famers Willie Mays and Willie McCovey.

Trainer Bob Bauman took credit for saying he hypnotized Washburn before the game and told him he was going to pitch a no-hitter. Still, the game was surprising for Washburn, but he was not surprised by the success the Cardinals enjoyed in 1967 and 1968.

"It was a self-motivating, self-disciplined club," Washburn said. "If somebody wasn't doing his job, other guys would let him know about it. Red (Schoendienst) kept everybody on their toes every day."

Washburn also is the answer to another trivia question. He was the Cardinals' starting pitcher in the first game at Busch Stadium on May 12, 1966, against Atlanta. He earned a no-decision in St. Louis's 4-3, 12-inning win.

He also was the winning pitcher in Game 3 of the 1968 World Series, a series he would like to forget as the Cardinals blew a three-one series lead, losing the final two games at home.

Following the 1969 season, Washburn was traded to Cincinnati and retired after spending the 1970 season with the Reds, where he did make it back to the World Series for the third time in his career. He was also with the Cardinals in 1964 but was not able to pitch because of his injury.

"Pitching in the World Series was the definite highlight of my career," Washburn said, "although I've tried to block 1968 out of my mind."

Where Have You Gone?

BOB TEWKSBURY

For many former major league players, the toughest challenge they face on a daily basis is whether the green on the 17th hole is breaking to the left or right. For Bob Tewksbury, the daily challenge in the fall of 2004 was whether to study *Adolescent Psychology* first, or the *Philosophies and Theories of Counseling*.

Tewksbury returned to school a couple of years ago to pursue his master's degree in sports psychology at Boston University, a task he completed in December 2004. He made the one-hour drive from his home in Concord, New Hampshire, to Boston a couple of times a week for classes.

"Going back to school when you are in your 40s, you see things a lot differently," Tewksbury said. "I love doing the research and the reading. The difficult part has been writing the papers, because it had been 18 years since I had done it."

Tewksbury's life has been anything but boring since he retired in spring training of 1999. He has spent five years working as a minor league pitching consultant for the Red Sox, which is what gave him the idea to pursue the advanced degree.

"I spent most of my time working away from the ballpark," Tewksbury said. "I had actually had a lot of conversations on the phone with guys. We talked about a lot more than just pitching."

In the five years since he retired, Tewksbury has also been the president of the Concord Little League, coached his son's teams, chaired

Gary Newkirk/Getty Images

BOB TEWKSBURY
Seasons with Cardinals: 1989-1994

Best season with Cardinals: 1992 (All-Star; third in N.L. Cy Young voting)

Games: 33 • Record: 16-5 (third in NL in wins)
ERA: 2.16 (second in NL) • IP: 233 (sixth in NL) • **Hits: 217**
BB/9IP: 0.77 (first in NL) • **SO: 91** • CG: 5

the county-wide United Way campaign that raised $2.1 million in 2001, instructed at baseball's annual rookie education program, and broadcast pre- and postgame television shows for the Red Sox during the 2004 season.

If that seems like he has had an easy transition to his life after his playing career came to an end, Tewksbury will argue that looks can be deceiving.

"It was a difficult transition, and I really didn't expect that," said Tewksbury. "I thought if I was just home with the kids I would be totally happy, but I found I needed a new carrot to keep me going. I needed to find something that gave me a little more fulfillment."

Tewksbury did find the extra time with his son Griffin, 13, and daughter Jenna, 11, enjoyable, but that alone did not fill the void created by not playing baseball.

"I didn't realize how much I identified my sense of self with being a ballplayer," Tewksbury said. "I didn't realize how much I was wrapped up into that. I didn't feel like there would be as big a void as I felt when I got out of the game.

"At this point I don't think I'm even over it, but I've learned how to handle it. That is a piece of you that will always be missing. The void will always be there. I'm trying to find a new passion. It's a constant work in progress for me. If I ever slow down, I will miss baseball again."

There doesn't appear to be a chance that Tewksbury will slow down any time soon. It's more a question of which activity is on the front burner at that particular moment.

"I am just riding whatever wave comes up," Tewksbury said.

Tewksbury gave up his broadcasting work for the 2005 season, agreeing to work as a coach for the Red Sox minor league system— working with the mental side of organizations players.

"I can see myself continuing to be very involved with my children's activities," Tewksbury said. "I kind of assemble my life around my wife and kids. Our focus is to get the kids prepared for school and to be successful in life."

Tewksbury has been able to combine his baseball work with the Red Sox with his class studies by working on a project that is trying to prove that pitch counts do not help prevent injuries.

He has examined data from 1992, the first year pitch count totals were readily available through 2001 and has come to the conclusion that more pitchers are getting hurt now and spending more time on the disabled list than they were in 1992.

"I think what it comes down to is that pitching is a high-risk activity," Tewksbury said. "I don't think there is any evidence that a pitch count, especially in pitchers 18 to 24, does anything to help prevent those injuries from occurring."

One casualty of Tewksbury's busy schedule has been his artwork, which brought him a lot of attention during his playing days with the Cardinals.

"The last thing I drew was in 1998, a picture of Mark McGwire and Ken Griffey Jr. for the Boys and Girls Club," Tewksbury said. "I've been too busy with other stuff. Once I get done with school I might have more free time to do that again."

The years he spent in St. Louis were the best of Tewksbury's career. He made his major league debut with the Yankees in 1986 and also pitched for the Cubs before joining the Cardinals in 1989. He was with the Cardinals through 1994, and finished his career with a season in Texas, a year in San Diego and two years in Minnesota.

Tewksbury's best two seasons came in 1992, when he went 16-5 with a 2.16 ERA and the following year, when he was 17-10. For his efforts in 1992, he finished third in the league in Cy Young voting after posting the second best ERA and the highest winning percentage in the league.

"It was my first chance to pitch without somebody looking over my shoulder," Tewksbury said. "[The Cardinals] didn't have a lot of success as a team, but we had some individual success. My son was born there, and I had my best season there. I will have those memories for a long time."

MIKE JORGENSEN

Mike Jorgensen was one of those players who knew he wanted to stay in baseball in some capacity when his playing career was over. His opportunity came just as he was retiring from the Cardinals before the 1986 season when a spot opened up for a minor league hitting instructor in the organization.

After playing in the major leagues for 15 years, he expected to make a very smooth transition to coaching younger players. It didn't take very long for Jorgensen to realize that would not be the case.

"Lee Thomas was the farm director and he told me, 'We have a kid from Venezuela who we think has a chance to be a pretty good player. We would like for you to work with him,'" Jorgensen recalled.

Jorgensen thought that seemed simple enough, and took a bag of baseballs with him to the field, ready to watch Jose Rocca hit off a batting T into a net.

"He missed the ball the first five swings off the T," Jorgensen said. "I had never seen anything like it. Playing in the major leagues for that many years makes you take so many things for granted. He never did make it."

That was the beginning of a career that has seen Jorgensen work as an instructor, minor league manager, field coordinator, director of player development, major league manager and special assistant to the general manager for the Cardinals over the past 18 years, a longer span than he wore the uniform as a player.

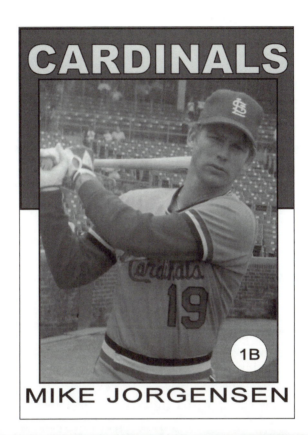

CARDINALS

1B

MIKE JORGENSEN

MIKE JORGENSEN
Seasons with Cardinals: 1984-1985

Best season with Cardinals: 1984

Games: 59 (as a Cardinal) • At-bats: 98 • BA: .245
OBP: .315 • HR: 1 • RBI: 12

"I've been really fortunate and am very grateful," Jorgensen said. "I've done a number of different things. I've seen the game from a lot of different angles, and it is still a beautiful game to me. The opportunity to work so many years in one organization is unusual, and I am thankful to the Cardinals."

Jorgensen's current assignment for the past two years is to work as a special assistant to general manager Walt Jocketty. His basic job is to scout two minor leagues and write reports on each of the players he observes, information the Cardinals will use if they are considering making a trade or when one of those players is called up to the major leagues and is going to play against the Cardinals. Last year he scouted the International League and the western half of the Southern League.

He has the freedom to set his own schedule, and that allows him to pack up his car, have his map ready and hit the road for the summer, armed with his schedule and hotel reservations.

"I enjoy that part of it," he said. "I enjoy watching baseball. Major league scouting is different—you have to do it a different way. When you go to watch minor league players, you really have to watch them for four or five days."

A lot of technical improvements have been made in the scouting profession in recent years. Now there's a greater reliance on computers, and different sets of statistics and methods of analysis are used to evaluate players. Jorgensen is in favor of anything that will increase the depth of knowledge of a player.

"When I was managing in Triple-A we still called in our game reports on the telephone," Jorgensen said. "Then the fax machine came into vogue and we sent the information back to St. Louis that way. I remember people thinking that was a fad which wouldn't last.

"Now everybody has a computer and all the reports are sent in that way. I know a lot of scouts who didn't want to learn how to use a computer. They also don't want to use a lot of the different statistics they have now, like OPS (on-base percentage plus slugging percentage). I love it.

"I ask questions about the guys who come up with stuff like that. I want to know how they came up with those numbers. I just look at it as another tool that will let us do a better job."

Jorgensen does not believe that computers and statistics will ever totally replace the personal aspect of scouting, especially when it comes to evaluating high school and college players in the amateur draft.

"I think it is especially important for an amateur scout to know what posters a kid has up in his room and what his relationship is with his mom and dad," Jorgensen said. "I think some of that information is actually more important than the raw numbers."

The biggest challenge Jorgensen has had since beginning his work in coaching and administration came in 1995, when he was called upon to replace Joe Torre as manager of the Cardinals in the middle of the season. He guided the team to a 41-55 record the rest of the season, while continuing his work as the director of player development. He returned to that job full-time when Tony La Russa was hired as manager.

"There were not enough hours in the day to do both," Jorgensen said.

Cardinal fans likely remember Jorgensen more from that assignment that they do as a Cardinals player. He spent only one and a half of his 15 seasons in St. Louis over the final year and a half of his career. He was traded to the Cardinals with Ken Dayley in exchange for Ken Oberkfell in 1984.

"I always thought it would be great to play in St. Louis when I was a visiting player and it *was* great," Jorgensen said. "Even though I was traded in the middle of the season I was happy about it.

"Being with the Cardinals gave me the only chance I had to play in the World Series. It really was a remarkable year. I wrote a diary of that season, starting in the middle of the year. I just ran across it when I was cleaning out some stuff in the basement. I didn't know I still had it."

One of the entries that stood out to Jorgensen was his entry after the seventh game loss in the World Series.

"I was really dissatisfied," Jorgensen said. "We didn't play that game. Like everyone else I was mad because we got screwed the night before, and after that happened it just looked like we expected to get beat."

Jorgensen, who moved to St. Louis when he became the director of player development, is the father of three grown children. He and wife Brenda's oldest son is a lawyer in Dallas, his daughter is teaching in Paris and his youngest son is in business in St. Louis. The Jorgensens also have a nine-year-old grandson.

Where Have You Gone?

ANDY VAN SLYKE

When he retired from the game, Andy Van Slyke had two desires—to find a way to stay involved in baseball, and also to spend more time with his family. He quickly found out the two were not very compatible.

"I always thought I would stay in the game in some way, and I haven't lost my desire to do that," Van Slyke said. "But if I had done that I would be missing a much more important thing in my life, and that's my relationship with my family. It just seems in baseball that the relationships with the people you are closest to are the ones which suffer the most."

Van Slyke was determined not to let that happen, which is why he has turned down opportunities to coach or manage in both the majors and minor leagues. He also turned down a chance to become one of the co-hosts on *The Best Damn Sports Show Period* on Fox because it would have meant a move or at least a commute to Los Angeles every week. He did spend one year working as a game analyst for ESPN, but decided it involved too great a time commitment.

Instead Van Slyke has maintained his baseball fix by working as an analyst on the postgame television shows after Cardinals games as well as co-hosting a weekly radio talk show during the season. In addition, he filled in for Mike Shannon as the analyst on several Cardinal broadcasts last season.

CARDINALS
ANDY VAN SLYKE
OUTFIELD

ANDY VAN SLYKE
Seasons with Cardinals: 1983-1986

Best season with Cardinals: 1986

Games: 137 • At-bats: 418 • BA: .270 • OBP: .343
SLG: .452 • HR: 13 • RBI: 61 • SB: 21

He also has spent a great deal of time working with his two oldest sons, A.J. and Scott, both of whom might be selected in the amateur baseball draft in June 2005. A.J. is a junior at the University of Kansas and Scott is a senior at John Burroughs High School in St. Louis. Scott also has accepted a scholarship to the University of Mississippi if he does not sign a professional contract.

Van Slyke intends to represent both of his sons in their possible contract negotiations with professional clubs with a rather unique approach.

"I won't be taking any of their income and putting the money in my back pocket," Van Slyke said. "And I really will have their best interests in mind. I really don't think Scott Boras has anybody's best interests in mind when he is negotiating a contract."

Whether he was a player or a broadcaster, Van Slyke has never been afraid to speak his mind and offer an opinion. It is a refreshing quality, but it has also got him in some controversial spots when he has criticized manager Tony La Russa.

La Russa was the manager when Van Slyke attempted to come back with the Cardinals in spring training 1997, after a year off, and some people have said his criticism of La Russa is personal, based on the fact that he did not make that ballclub.

"The only place I wanted to play was St. Louis, and the most disappointing thing was how hard I had worked to get in shape and I had really worked hard on changing my swing. I hit .525 that spring but got hurt right at the end of camp and that was it," Van Slyke said.

"People who think it is personal don't understand me, they don't understand the situation and they don't understand Tony La Russa. It never has been personal. I make an observation based on his thinking or decisions. My comments have nothing to do with Tony's personality. I said some things about Phil Garner in the playoffs last year and nobody said that was personal."

In reality, Van Slyke has a lot of respect for La Russa as a manager and believes he belongs in the Hall of Fame.

"I never like to say someone is the greatest player or the greatest manager, but he is a great manager," Van Slyke said. "His work ethic is the most respectable thing about him and the thing I admire most about him."

Van Slyke played for two other "great" managers in his career, Whitey Herzog with the Cardinals and Jim Leyland with the Pirates. He broke into the majors with the Cardinals in 1983 and was traded to the Pirates with Mike LaValliere for Tony Pena on April Fool's Day 1987. He thought his teammates were playing a joke on him until he was called into Herzog's office.

As much as he did not want to leave St. Louis, the move was good for him. Van Slyke got the chance to play every day that he never had, and never thought he would get, with the Cardinals. He became a three-time All-Star, won five Gold Gloves and just missed helping the Pirates get to the World Series in three consecutive years, losing each time in the NLCS.

He peaked in St. Louis in 1986, when he hit 13 homers for the second consecutive year and increased his RBI total from 55 to 61. Playing full time with the Pirates, Van Slyke's best year was 1988, when he scored 101 runs, led the league with 15 triples, hit 25 homers and drove in 100 runs. He also finished second in the league in batting in 1992 with a .324 mark to go along with 89 RBIs.

Van Slyke's family considered moving full time to Pittsburgh. He knows he would have had many more post-career opportunities there than he has had in St. Louis, but Van Slyke has never regretted his family's decision to keep their permanent home in St. Louis.

"We had put roots down here and had a lot of close friends and really liked St. Louis, so we decided to stay," Van Slyke said.

Partially because he never had the on-field success in St. Louis that he had in Pittsburgh, Van Slyke didn't achieve the same level of popularity with the Cardinals that he did with the Pirates.

"In three and a half years in St. Louis I never had the opportunity to be an everyday player," Van Slyke said. "I never have quite understood how it's okay for a switch-hitter to hit .220 against left-handers but it isn't okay for a lefthanded hitter to hit .220 against left-handers, even if he is hitting .360 against righthanders. It's tough to get a hit when you are sitting on the bench. It's a pretty bad angle."

When he isn't talking about the Cardinals, pitching batting practice to his sons, or spending time with wife Lauri or his younger sons, Jared and Nathan, Van Slyke likely can be found on a golf course somewhere. He is a member of the Celebrity Players Tour and has a goal of winning his first tournament in 2005. He has finished second and third, but has never won.

"It's a great release for me," he said. "It's so uniquely different than baseball."

Van Slyke also is involved in writing a baseball novel, a project he has wanted to do for several years.

"I really don't have any future long-term plans," he said. "I wish I could still be young enough to play and have all the kids grown up and gone, but I know that isn't going to happen."

Where Have You Gone?

ERNIE BROGLIO

Forty-one years later, Ernie Broglio knows his baseball legacy will forever be that he was the principal player the Chicago Cubs acquired when they traded Lou Brock to the Cardinals. He also is happy to let the world know that he is okay with that.

At the time of the June 15, 1964 trade, most observers thought the Cubs got the better end of the trade. Broglio was a proven righthanded starting pitcher, who at age 29, figured to be headed for several more good years similar to the 18-win, 2.99 ERA season he had posted in 1963.

There were four other players involved in the deal, two on each side, but the two principles were Brock and Broglio. And while Brock went on to establish himself as a Hall of Famer, Broglio came down with a sore arm, won only seven more games in his career and was out of baseball after 1966.

"I had an elbow operation in November (1965) and was back trying to pitch again in spring training," Broglio said. "Pitchers today have the same surgery and are out for a year and a half. I didn't even think about it, because in those days the ballclub's investment in its players was not as enormous. They didn't take the steps they take today to protect their players.

"You had a different outlook on the game, because they knew if you didn't perform they had somebody waiting to take your place."

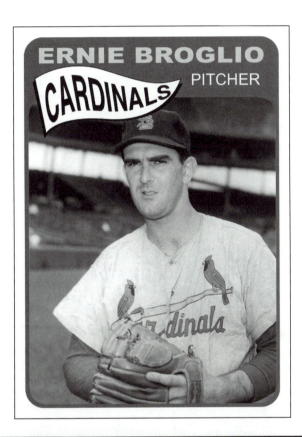

ERNIE BROGLIO
Seasons with Cardinals: 1959-1964

Best season with Cardinals: 1960
(third in Cy Young voting; ninth in NL MVP voting)
Games: 52 • Record: 21-9 (first in wins in NL)
ERA: 2.74 (second in NL) • IP: 226.3 • Hits: 172
SO: 188 (fourth in NL) • BB: 100 • CG: 9 • SHO: 3 (eighth in NL)

Cardinals general manager Bing Devine, who engineered the trade, admitted he had no idea it would turn out the way it did. All he was trying to do was give his seventh-place team a spark, which Brock definitely provided.

The deal initially was more popular in Chicago than in St. Louis, where Broglio's ex-Cardinal teammates were generally of the opinion that the team had given up too much in exchange for the unproven Brock.

"Broglio was a 20-game winner," said catcher Tim McCarver. "We couldn't believe we'd give up a quality pitcher for an unproven guy like Lou Brock. But it didn't take long."

Added first baseman Bill White, "I didn't think it was a good trade. Most of us were upset. We traded three guys for a guy who was very raw and didn't know how to play. I didn't like it. If anybody tells you they approved of that trade, they're lying."

Devine, of course, did not stick around long enough to see Brock help the Cardinals win the pennant and the World Series. He was fired by owner Gussie Busch in August of 1964; Busch believed the Cardinals were going to continue their pennant-less streak, a drought that had endured since 1946.

What upset Broglio about the trade was not that he was dealt for a future Hall of Famer, it was that he was traded at all. The Cardinals had acquired him from the Giants before the 1959 season and he spent five years in St. Louis, becoming attached to his teammates and the organization.

"I didn't want to leave because it was a lot of fun there," Broglio said. "The organization and Mr. Busch treated you like a human being. There was not the same atmosphere around the Cubs. I also was not the greatest fan of day baseball. As a pitcher I always thought it was easier for the hitters to see the ball during the day.

"It hurt even more when the Cardinals won the World Series (in 1964). A lot of the players called me from their party at Stan Musial's restaurant after the last game. They passed the phone around, and I really appreciated it. I popped open my own bottle of champagne and drank along with them.

"I looked at it like they won the pennant by one game, and I won [three games] for the Cardinals that year before I was traded, so I thought I had helped them win it."

Unlike today, when anybody who played for a championship team during the season is eligible for a share of the postseason money and a ring, Broglio received neither, and said he never thought about it.

"It would have been nice to have a ring, but I didn't get one, so I didn't worry about it," he said.

Broglio set his attention on his life after baseball, supporting his wife and four kids. He had spent the winters during his playing career working for a liquor warehouse and was able to expand that into a full-time job when he retired.

He also kept involved in baseball by working as a pitching coach for a local high school and for Santa Clara University for several years, in addition to giving private lessons. Now 69 years old, he still gives lessons to several youngsters in the Bay Area.

What he shares with them is not pitching advice, but instructions on how to throw a baseball properly—whether you are an outfielder or a pitcher. When he isn't doing that or playing golf, he is most likely spending time with his children and grandchildren, all of whom live within a couple of hours of San Jose. Broglio still lives in the same house he moved into in 1959.

"Barbara and I just celebrated our 50th wedding anniversary," Broglio said in November 2004. "The kids gave us a trip up to the wine country in Napa Valley for the weekend, and we had a wonderful time."

Broglio and Brock often appear together at autograph shows, and he even has his own autographed photo of Brock hanging on a wall in his den.

"As long as people remember him, I know they also are going to remember me," Broglio said.

RICK HORTON

Rick Horton retired from baseball in 1991 when he realized no team wanted his services. He wasn't certain what he wanted to do with the rest of his life, so he spent close to a year exploring a variety of options, including spending a day with then-Missouri governor John Ashcroft to find out what that job was like.

"I was with him from 6 a.m. to 6 p.m. and I came away convinced that was not the job for me," Horton says. "But I did look into a lot of things … coaching, broadcasting, politics, business, engineering. I went on a lot of job interviews. It was a great process.

"And I still maintain a lot of interest in several of those things, especially broadcasting."

Horton pitched for the Cardinals from 1984 to 1987 and again in 1989-1990. He was used primarily as a reliever by the Cardinals during the mid and late 1980s, combining with Ken Dayley to form a reliable lefthanded duo.

He also filled in as a starter during his first few seasons in St. Louis, combining for 36 career starts between 1984 and 1987. When he wasn't starting, he was used most often as a setup man, recording only 13 career saves in a Cardinal uniform.

Horton was traded to the White Sox before the 1988 season, along with outfielder Lance Johnson, in exchange for starting pitcher Jose DeLeon. Horton moved on from the White Sox to the Dodgers in time to become a member of their 1988 World Championship team.

RICK HORTON
Seasons with Cardinals: 1984-1987; 1989-1990

Best season with Cardinals: 1986

Games: **42** • Record: **4-3** • ERA: **2.24** • IP: **100.3**
Hits: **77** • SO: **49** • BB: **26** • SV: **3**

After retiring, Horton spent one season working as a minor league pitching coach for the Indians, but realized that job was taking him away from his family—wife Ann, daughter Jennifer and son Drew—too much. He explored other possibilities and settled in a job he thinks might have been created for him in Heaven.

For his "day" job, Horton was hired in 1993 to run the operations for the St. Louis area chapter of the Fellowship of Christian Athletes, a position he has held ever since.

"I went to my first FCA meeting when I was in college, and I was lucky enough to experience FCA as a professional athlete, as a volunteer and as a board member. I worked the camps. It just so happened that at the time, Walt Enoch, who had run the St. Louis chapter for years, was looking to step back from some of his responsibilities. I thought I wanted to get the job as the baseball coach at Washington University (in St. Louis) but I didn't get that job."

Instead, he wound up working with the FCA, which has allowed him to remain connected with athletes, working as a chapel leader with the Cardinals and the Rams, as well as working with numerous high schools in the St. Louis area.

"I'm not just hanging around watching games," Horton says. "There are a lot of different aspects to the job such as leadership, fundraising and the business side, and coaching the coaches. There is a lot of work that goes on behind the scenes that people don't see."

The most difficult period of Horton's time with the FCA was the June day in 2002 when he got the news that Cardinal pitcher Darryl Kile had been found dead in his hotel room in Chicago. Horton was in St. Louis, and was told the ballclub wanted him to join the team in Chicago immediately.

Horton found it very difficult to counsel the players and their families through that tragedy.

"I caught myself thinking 'What I am doing here? What do I know about this?' I thought I was way out of my league. But then I thought, 'If not me, who?'"

Horton knows God gave him the strength to get through that period of mourning, which he still believes has not ended for those who were the closest to Kile.

"I had a relationship with everybody involved, and I needed to be there," Horton said. "I didn't feel equipped to do it, but I kind of felt like I was the person who was supposed to do it."

Luckily for Horton, his "normal" days are much more fun and involve a lot less stress than dealing with that kind of challenge. He works with many local coaches and athletes, especially on the high school level, about what it means to be a Christian coach or athlete. He finds there are always more coaches or athletes to talk to than he has time available.

One of the current challenges at the FCA office is trying to decide whether they are going to rebuild a camp near Cuba, Missouri, which burned down in 2001. Former Cardinal Todd Worrell is in charge of the fundraising efforts, and the board will soon make a decision on which direction they want to take, Horton said.

"It's been a long, slow process with a lot of different options," Horton said. "We have to decide what is the best way to go about getting a facility which best meets our needs."

Since the fire, the FCA has been hosting its camps at different locations, which has not been an ideal solution. There is a possibility the FCA may partner with another organization in building a new camp, or they may decide to own the camp outright. The goal is not to make money on the camp, but not to have it be a drain on the association's other resources either.

When he is not fulfilling his FCA duties, Horton has worked for the past several seasons as a broadcaster for the Cardinals on both television and radio, an arrangement he truly loves. In 2004 he was the analyst on games televised by KPLR, Channel 11, usually on the weekends, and he will fill the same role in 2005. He moves over to the radio side to fill-in when Mike Shannon goes on vacation.

His first broadcast assignment came in 1997, when he worked three games in Atlanta. "My first game Alan Benes had a no-hitter going into the ninth inning," Horton recalled. "I really felt the pressure of the job."

Horton intends to keep doing both jobs as long as possible. His schedule has allowed him to follow the careers of his children as well, with Jennifer playing volleyball and basketball and Drew participating in soccer.

"I get to go on weekend trips, stay at a Ritz-Carlton and watch baseball games and get paid for it," Horton said. "What's not to like about that? And then I get to come home and take out the trash and become a normal person again."

Where Have You Gone?

PAT PERRY

Even though he has been out of professional baseball for 10 years, Pat Perry has not lost his disappointment or his bitterness about how his career came to an end.

He still is angry about the way he was treated by Don Zimmer and the Chicago Cubs, by Tommy Lasorda and the Dodgers, by Buck Rodgers and the Angels and by Bob Boone and the Kansas City Royals. At one time or another, all were involved in releasing Perry when he thought he still was able to pitch.

"When it ended, I didn't think I was done," Perry said. "I will probably always carry that bitterness with me. I had a lot of sour feelings. I had about a 10-year hangover coming out of baseball. I really did a lot of searching to figure out what I was supposed to do. Somebody with only one year of college doesn't have much appeal to a lot of people."

Perry has settled down into a very steady business of giving pitching lessons to kids in the St. Louis area. Now remarried and the father of four children under the age of seven, with a fifth due in 2005, Perry has more than enough in his life to keep him quite active.

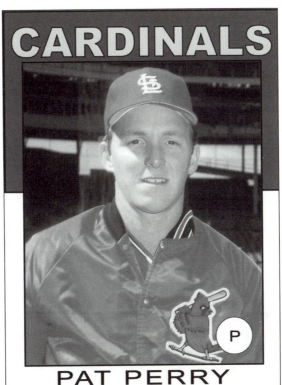

PAT PERRY
Seasons with Cardinals: 1985-1987

Best season with Cardinals: 1986

Games: **46** • Record: **2-3** • ERA: **3.80** • IP: **68.7**
Hits: **59** • SO: **29** • BB: **34** • SV: **2**

"I really enjoy working with the kids," Perry said. "Teaching is the one thing that really made sense to me the same way that playing baseball made sense. I know where I stand with the kids and their parents."

A native of Taylorville, Illinois, Perry didn't always feel that way about many of the people he was involved with in professional baseball, especially after he left the Cardinals. Perry was with the Cardinals from 1985 through 1987, leaving when he was traded to the Cincinnati Reds for Scott Terry. He began to see his baseball career go downhill the following year when he was traded by the Reds to the Cubs for Leon Durham. His last major league season was 1990, when he pitched for the Dodgers.

A lefthanded reliever, Perry was used almost exclusively in middle-inning roles by the Cardinals. In his three seasons with St. Louis he pitched in 97 games and recorded three saves.

Perry thought he would have a chance to continue that role with both the Reds and the Cubs, until he had his first run-in with Zimmer, then managing the Cubs. That led to Perry tearing his rotator cuff.

"I will go to my grave never figuring out what happened," Perry said. "It was in spring training against the Giants, and I gave up a hit to Robby Thompson. It was something like an 11-pitch at-bat and he just flared one over Mark Grace's head. We ended up losing the game, and I didn't pitch again for the last two weeks of spring training. Neither did Jeff Pico.

"We both still made the team, and it was the second game of the season and it was a really cold game. I pitched three perfect innings but I had no arm strength. I was surprised I pitched that well. Then [Zimmer] sent me out for another inning and I got in trouble."

After the game, the reporters asked Perry about his performance, and he explained how he had tired in the fourth inning. He asked the reporters to find out from Zimmer why he had not pitched for more than two weeks. The next day, Zimmer came looking for Perry in the locker room.

"He still didn't really have an answer about why I hadn't pitched, but he said I was going to have to work my way out of his doghouse. I still couldn't figure out why I was in his doghouse," Perry said.

Motivated, Perry went on a streak of 22 consecutive scoreless innings before a game in New York, when he tried to drop down and throw a sidearm pitch to Dave Magadan and tore his rotator cuff.

The problems with Zimmer and the Cubs persisted to the point where it took several months before Perry underwent surgery, and the lingering affects of that stayed with him for the next several years.

He was released by the Cubs and signed with Los Angeles, where he tried to come back within six months of the surgery. He pitched through pain, and lost a game in Pittsburgh that upset Lasorda.

"He came in the locker room after the game and sat everybody down and just walked around for 30 minutes, cursing non-stop," Perry said. "It was unbelievable. It seemed like it lasted for three hours. I felt terrible, but my arm was killing me. That shut me back down again. Everything I had worked so hard for had blown up in my face."

The Dodgers wanted to take Perry off the roster, but still re-sign him that winter, but Perry refused and became a free agent. The best offer he could get was a Triple-A deal with the Phillies.

That launched a stretch in which Perry failed to garner interest from the big leagues, and included a spring training invitation with the Angels and a Triple-A contract with the Padres. He thought he had a chance in 1995 when he joined the Royals as one of their replacement players in spring training. He was told he would be called up by the major league team after some time in Triple-A but instead was released.

"Being a replacement player might have been the underlying reason," Perry said. "They had told me I was going to be pitching with them and was going to be called up and instead I got released."

That was Perry's final attempt to make it back to the major leagues.

"Baseball had been my whole life," he said. "I didn't know if I was supposed to do something else. I'm lucky the teaching has worked out. I really enjoy it almost as much as I did playing.

"And at least I know where I stand."

Where Have You Gone?

RAY CUNNINGHAM

The search for the oldest living major leaguer, who happens to be a former Cardinal, ended in a nursing home in Pearland, Texas, outside of Houston, where Ray Cunningham celebrated his 100th birthday on January 17, 2005.

Cunningham was tracked down through the efforts of Brian Walton of TheStlCardinals.com and Bill McCurdy, an official of the Texas Baseball Hall of Fame. They located Cunningham at the Windsong Village Convalescent Home. McCurdy went and visited him last fall.

Cunningham, who goes by the name Lee as well as Ray, has become much more famous in his post-baseball life than he ever did as a player for the Cardinals. His major league career consisted of 14 games, three in 1931 and 11 in 1932, all as the third baseman for the Cardinals. He was four for 26 at the plate in his brief career.

When 99-year-old Paul Hopkins died early in 2004, researchers determined Cunningham was the oldest living ex-major leaguer. He received a letter wishing him a happy birthday from commissioner Bud Selig.

McCurdy reported that Cunningham was very much alert and still a big baseball fan. He admitted his loyalties were divided when his two favorite teams, the Cardinals and Astros, met in the NLCS in 2004 with a berth in the World Series at stake.

RAY CUNNINGHAM
Seasons with Cardinals: 1931-1932

Best season with Cardinals: 1932

Games: 11 • At-bats: 22 • BA: .182 • R: 4

"I have fond memories of my days with the Cardinals, but I'm a Houstonian now and I've become a big Astros fan over the years," Cunningham said.

Cunningham said the only reason he has lived such a long life is "just my good luck. Nobody can count on living as long as I have. It either happens or it doesn't."

Cunningham was the youngest of five boys and worked on the family farm as he grew up and began playing baseball. He signed with the Cardinals out of high school and began his minor league career in 1926.

"I loved everything about playing baseball," Cunningham told McCurdy. "It was just a thing I put my whole heart into. The way I figured it, I didn't want to put my life into anything that my heart was not up to following, too. Baseball filled the bill for me."

Cunningham hit .311 or better in each of his first three years in the minors, making the Central League All-Star team at Dayton in 1928.

"I was a little guy (five foot seven, 140 pounds) in my playing days and not a power threat, but I could hit line drives that found a way of falling in," Cunningham said.

Cunningham made his major-league debut with the Cardinals on September 16, 1931, going zero for four. After his short stint with the team in 1932, he was sent back to the minor leagues, to Houston, and soon made the decision to retire.

"I quit baseball to take a job with the Grand Prize Brewery in Houston," Cunningham said. "As much as I loved baseball, the beer business paid better and I needed the money."

Cunningham stayed with the brewery until he retired. He and wife Dorothy, who died about a month before their 50th wedding anniversary, had one son, Lee, and Cunningham also has two grandsons and two great-grandsons.

Even though he did not recall the specific details of his major-league debut, Cunningham did say that Jim Bottomley and Joe Medwick were his favorite hitters on the Cardinals of that era, and he also liked Met Ott of the Giants. His favorite player of all, however, was Dizzy Dean.

"Diz and me were roommates for a short time with the Cardinals," Cunningham said. "He was a whole lot of fun to be with. He didn't put on no airs and heck, he just liked to go out and have some fun. Back in 1932, so did I. I'll always be glad to know that I once played ball with one of the greatest pitchers of all time."

Cunningham's fondest memory in baseball is little more than a sketch, McCurdy said, and he cannot recall when or where it happened. But the play is crystal clear in his mind.

"It was a close game in the late innings," Cunningham said. "I was playing third base and the other team had an important runner there. We had to keep him from scoring. The next thing I knew, the batter hit a hard line smash at me that I managed to knock down with the heel of my glove. The runner had been going for home, but he stopped for a moment to look at me when the ball got hit. Then he took off again when he saw the ball bounce to the ground. That was his mistake. I pounced on that ball with my bare hand and winged it like a bullet to our catcher. That runner slid right into a surefire out."

More than 70 years after that play, Cunningham still gets as excited telling the story as he was the day it actually occurred.

JOHN TUDOR

John Tudor's competitive fire is still on display these days, but you have to go to a hockey rink to find it.

During his baseball career, especially his years in St. Louis, Tudor was as fierce a competitor as one could find. He had a quick and biting wit, and when he believed it was warranted, he unleashed it on unsuspecting targets, often members of the media.

One of his most infamous remarks came during the 1985 postseason, when he was complaining about the increased media coverage for the Cardinals and he asked, "What does it take to get a media pass, a driver's license?"

Cardinal fans identified with Tudor because he was proof positive that a pitcher did not have to possess a 100-mph fastball in order to be effective. The key to his success was almost pinpoint control and an ability to mix up his pitches and force hitters to get themselves out more often than not. Tudor was also was a master of never wasting pitches, which allowed him to continually pitch deep into games.

The 1985 season was Tudor's finest year in the major leagues, coming in his first season after being traded to the Cardinals from Pittsburgh for outfielder George Hendrick. He led the Cardinals to the NL pennant by going 21-8 in the regular season with an eye-popping 1.93 ERA. He pitched 14 complete games, including a league-high 10 shutouts. He also led the league in fewest hits plus walks allowed per nine innings, at 8.44.

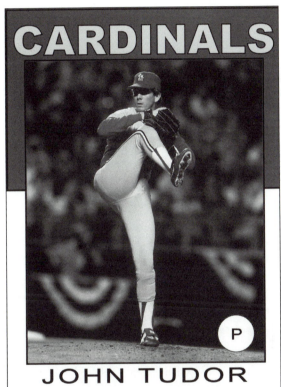

Focus on Sport/Getty Images

JOHN TUDOR
Seasons with Cardinals: 1985-1988; 1990

Best season with Cardinals: 1985
(second in Cy Young voting; eighth in MVP voting)

Games: 36 • Record: 21-8 (second in wins in NL) • ERA: 1.93 (second in NL) • IP: 275 (second in NL) • Hits: 209 • SO: 169 (sixth in NL) BB: 49 • CG: 14 (second in NL) • SHO: 10 (first in NL)

The most remarkable part of his performance in 1985 was that on May 29, his record stood at 1-7. He proceeded to win 20 of his next 21 starts, losing only to the Dodgers' Fernando Valenzuela when the Cardinals were shut out.

On the national stage, however, he is remembered more as the starting and losing pitcher in Game 7 of the World Series to Kansas City. The night after Don Denkinger's blown call at first base helped force the seventh game, Tudor was knocked out in the third inning after allowing three runs. Two more runs scored against reliever Bill Campbell and were charged to Tudor, putting the Cardinals in a 5-0 hole after three innings.

When he left the game, he took out his anger and frustration on a metal fan, cutting his hand and requiring a trip to the hospital. Nearly 20 years later, Tudor has no trouble remembering that game, for all the wrong reasons.

"Of all the days to suck," Tudor says. "We were having trouble scoring runs, and the last thing we wanted was to be out of the game early. We were not going to come back and score five or six runs. It would have made a difference if we had stayed in the game early. It was just too bad that it worked out that way."

Tudor and the Cardinals got another chance in the World Series two years later, but again lost, this time to Minnesota. He finally got his championship ring in 1988 after being traded by the Cardinals to the Dodgers in August for Pedro Guerrero.

"I was disappointed and surprised," Tudor says of the trade. "I was getting phone calls to get my reaction before I was officially told I was traded. But it gave me a chance to go over there and win a world championship, which didn't happen in St. Louis. The Dodgers were a good team with a good group of guys.

"Then I got a chance to come back and play my last season in St. Louis [in 1990], so it was kind of the best of both worlds."

Tudor still possesses the best winning percentage for his career of any Cardinal pitcher, at .705. His 1.93 ERA in 1985 is still the second best mark for a season in team history, trailing only Bob Gibson's mark of 1.12 in 1968.

Tudor retired after the 1990 season with no major plans to speak of. He has dabbled in coaching, spending a year in the minors with the Cardinals, a year with the Phillies and a couple of seasons with the Texas Rangers, but spends most of his time these days close to his wife and three children and his suburban Boston home.

Thirteen-year-old Allison and 11-year-old twins Casey and Corey are very active in sports and activities, and Tudor tries to spend as much time with them as possible. He has coached the twins' baseball and hockey teams for several years.

Hockey was Tudor's first love when he was growing up, and he still remains active in the sport. He plays in a couple adult recreation leagues around Boston during the winter, averaging about three games a week.

Asked what the difference was between him as a baseball player and a hockey player, Tudor responded, "skill level. I'm not as skilled a hockey player, but I really enjoy the game. It's always been my first love."

Tudor played junior varsity hockey in high school. Surprisingly, for someone who celebrated a 50th birthday in 2004, Tudor still enjoys the physical activity.

"It's the one thing my body still lets me do," said Tudor. "When I broke my leg, that kept me from running or jumping too much, so playing hockey is pretty much about all I can do."

Tudor remains a fan of baseball as well. He and his family spent several days in St. Louis in 2004 and he said his boys had a great time seeing where their dad had played and meeting several of his former teammates.

Tudor is not a fan of the way the game is run these days, particularly as the parent of two young boys who often could not attend or watch their favorite Red Sox win the World Series because the games were on so late at night.

"We don't go in to watch games that much here," Tudor said. "Fenway is just not as fan friendly a place to watch a game as St. Louis. Everybody stands up and screams at the Yankees and the kids can't see. You just don't find that kind of atmosphere in St. Louis.

"I was really disappointed with the playoffs and the World Series, with the way TV treats the games. They didn't start until 8:20 at night and the Red Sox didn't clinch the last game until about 11:30 on a school night. I took the boys to one of the playoff games against the Yankees and they were asleep in their seats by the fourth inning. It was 11 o'clock at night."

Tudor knows he likely has little chance of changing baseball's relationship with television, so he is more focused on helping raise his kids. He still does not plan too far into the future, although he has realized he will have three kids in college at the same time in a few years.

"That's kind of scary," he says. "I really didn't have any preconceived notions about what my life after baseball was going to be like, but it has worked out pretty well."

Where Have You Gone?

TOM PAGNOZZI

Tom Pagnozzi is one of the few players over the past two decades who spent his entire career—minors and majors—in one organization. Pagnozzi had been selected by the Milwaukee Brewers in the 1982 draft but did not sign. He was then drafted by the Cardinals the following year and appeared in 927 games for St. Louis between 1987 and 1998.

Pagnozzi was named an All-Star in 1992 and was a three-time Gold Glove winner in 1991, 1992 and 1994. His best offensive season came in 1996, when he hit 13 homers and drove in 55 runs while posting a .270 average.

But when it came time to hang up his spikes in 1998, Pagnozzi did what a lot of people do when they retire—he moved to Arizona.

Pagnozzi, who had grown up in Tucson, moved to Paradise Valley, a suburb of Phoenix, and settled into what he thought would be a comfortable life of "not doing anything" except being involved in his kids' activities, playing golf and watching baseball on television. He also bought season tickets for Diamondbacks' games.

He found out, however, that reality was different that his expectations.

"We didn't like Phoenix as much as we thought we would," Pagnozzi said. "It was not a good environment for raising kids. We were living behind iron gates."

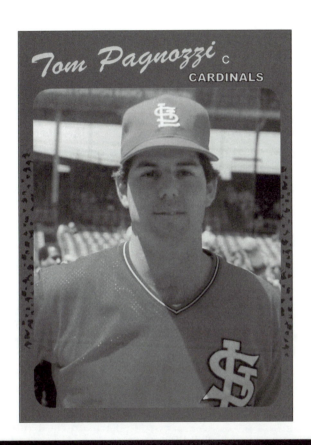

TOM PAGNOZZI
Seasons with Cardinals: 1987-1998

Best season with Cardinals: 1996

Games: 119 • At-bats: 407 • BA: .270 • 2B: 23
HR: 13 • RBI: 55 • R: 48

Three years was enough for Pagnozzi and his family, who moved two years ago to Fayetteville, Arkansas, where he lived when he was going to school and playing baseball at the University of Arkansas. He and his family, including daughters Tiffany and Brittany, 14 and 13, and son Andy, 8, are all much happier now.

"We thought about moving back to St. Louis at one point," Pagnozzi said. "It was as hot as hell in Arizona. I don't remember it being that hot when I was a kid. I don't know how I played in it. We missed the four seasons and we missed the St. Louis type of people."

The move to Fayetteville came about when Dave Van Horn, a college teammate of Pagnozzi's, was hired as the Razorbacks' new baseball coach. He encouraged Pagnozzi to move back to the area and work with the team as a volunteer assistant.

Pagnozzi did that for the past two years, but since he was a volunteer and not officially on the coaching staff, there were many restrictions placed on what he could and could not legally do.

He spent a lot of time working with the players and letting them hang out at his house, but he just found he was putting in too much time for what he was able to get out of the work.

"I enjoyed it tremendously, and I still see the kids all the time," Pagnozzi said. "I could not be involved in recruiting off campus, and we could only work with four kids at a time out of season. I was helping out in the weight room, and I was there from six in the morning to four or six in the afternoon. They are only allowed to receive eight hours of instruction a week, so they had to come in between classes. That made for a long day."

The team did have success, earning a trip to the College World Series in Omaha in 2004.

"It's different now than when I played," Pagnozzi said. "The pitching is not as deep. Players are bigger and stronger. I don't think they are better players; I think the players in my day were more fundamentally sound."

Pagnozzi is still keeping his eyes on the Arkansas squad while running a new business he formed a little more than a year ago, building homes in the Fayetteville area with his brother-in-law, Norm Wilcoxson, who had been working for another home builder in Arizona before moving to Arkansas.

"This is a growing area with a lot of money," Pagnozzi said. "It's a lot like the Scottsdale area was 20 years ago. *Forbes Magazine* ranked it as one of the top five places to live in America."

The business is off to a great start, he said.

"My job is more in the financial area of things," he said, "acquiring the land and things like that. I do go to a worksite almost every day and get on a tractor and do whatever they need me to do. I'm learning the business, but I really don't want to be doing it 40 to 60 hours a week. But it is giving me something to do and keeping me busy."

When he isn't working on watching the Razorbacks, Pagnozzi is closely following the Cardinals. He was glad the team had the success it did in 2004 and believes the future will be exciting for several years to come.

"My best memory there was going to the 1987 World Series," he said. "It was an incredible experience as a rookie. What was most incredible to me over the years was the commitment of the fans. There isn't a better baseball town anywhere. They really support their club.

"When they get a good team like they've got right now they really are something else. That team is going to be dangerous for the next three or four years."

When he lived in Arizona, Pagnozzi had one room in his house outfitted with five televisions, which often would be tuned to different baseball games, starting as early as 10 o'clock in the morning. He wants to have a similar setup in his new house he is building on four acres just outside of Fayetteville.

The 42-year-old Pagnozzi admits that in the next few years, he might be looking at baseball from a different perspective, from the dugout of a minor league franchise.

"Every year I inch closer and closer to getting back in it," he said. "I got a couple of offers while I was in Arizona, but I wasn't ready then. The only place I really want to work is for the Cardinals, so we will just have to see what happens."

Where Have You Gone?

KEN DAYLEY

K en Dayley was one of the Cardinals' most reliable relievers during the 1980s after joining the team in the middle of the 1984
season in the trade with Atlanta that sent third baseman Ken
Oberkfell to the Braves. Manager Whitey Herzog immediately put
Dayley to work in the bullpen where the lefthander became a valu-
able setup man for the next several years.

He was a key component in the Cardinals' bullpen by committee
that replaced closer Bruce Sutter, and he was a big reason behind the
team's successful pennant-winning years in both 1985 and 1987. He
recorded 11 saves in 1985 and had 12 saves in 1989.

Dayley left the Cardinals as a free agent after the 1990 season and
signed with the Toronto Blue Jays, where his career took a turn for
the worse. Dayley knew his life after baseball would always be affected by what happened to him while he was playing the game, but he
never knew that would literally be the case.

He was with the Blue Jays near the end of spring training in 1991,
shagging fly balls in the outfield during batting practice, when the
ball began to look "funny" to him.

"It was kind of getting ahead of my eyes, and they were having to
jump to catch up with it," Dayley recalled. "Then I was playing
catch, and found out I was having to jump at the ball to catch it. I
thought, 'This is really weird.'

"The next day I came out to the mound to pitch, against the
Phillies, and Rod Booker was the first batter. I remember going into

CARDINALS

KEN DAYLEY

P

Otto Greule Jr./Getty Images

KEN DAYLEY
Seasons with Cardinals: 1984-1990

Best season with Cardinals: 1987

Games: 53 • Record: 9-5 • ERA: 2.66 • IP: 61
Hits: 52 • SO: 63 • BB: 33 • SV: 4

my motion and feeling real unstable with my leg kick. I let go of the pitch and then I didn't know what happened. I heard the crowd oohing. When I got to where I could focus, I saw Booker laying on his back. Greg Myers was the catcher, and I called him out. By this time the folks in the dugout knew something was wrong and Cito (Gaston, the manager) came out too.

"I told him I just felt dizzy and something wasn't right. They took me out of the game and to the hospital. I never had the complete spinning sensation, but everything was kind of moving. It all happened over about a 24-hour period."

Dayley found out later that he was suffering from a severe case of vertigo, one that effectively ended his career. Dayley pitched only 10 games for Toronto, eight in 1991 and two in 1993, covering a total of five innings. He tried one comeback in the minor leagues with the Dodgers, but quickly concluded that it wasn't going to work out. He was forced to retire.

Dayley spent significant time being examined by doctors all over the U.S. and Canada in an attempt to discover the cause of his vertigo. He learned that about 70 to 75 percent of people suffer the kind of vertigo that goes away in a few days. His case was different, and what the doctors finally determined was the most likely cause stemmed from when he contracted meningitis in 1986. That virus stayed dormant until it moved out and traumatized a nerve years later.

"Nerves are about the only thing they can't seem to fix these days," Dayley said.

Dayley went through various types of treatment, which made his condition better even though it never completely went away. He was actually pitching well in spring training of 1993 when a hurricane came through Florida.

"That put me right back where I was (before)," Dayley said. "What we found was that sudden changes in barometric pressure really affect it."

The vertigo kept him from pitching, and more importantly now, has stayed with Dayley even after his playing career came to an end. More than 10 years later, he knows that is likely never going to change.

"It's there every day," Dayley says. "I've learned there are things I can do and things I can't do. I've had to adapt to it. I'm not under any medication, because there really is nothing they can do for it.

"I've found out there are a lot of things that affect it—too much salt or alcohol makes it worse, not enough sleep. A lot of things magnify the unstableness. I know I can't carry heavy stuff above my shoulders. Ladders are not a good idea. I've found I am visually dependent on light. I need something I can focus on."

For about the first two years after he returned home, Dayley said he felt like a counselor because so many people were calling him for advice about what to do with their bouts of vertigo.

"People thought they were losing their minds because they couldn't figure out what was happening to them," Dayley said.

Dayley has not let his condition affect his love for hunting, but it has forced him to make some extra accommodations.

"Walking to the tree stand, because of the unstableness of the ground and terrain, it might be 50 steps to get there and it might take me 150 steps," he said.

Dayley goes hunting as often as he can with his son, most often for deer or turkey near his St. Louis home, or for pheasants or ducks in South Dakota. He often hunts on land he owns in southern Missouri.

For the past dozen years, Dayley has earned his income by buying farms in southern Missouri, harvesting the wood on the farms and then breaking up the farms and re-selling them. "I've always wanted land, but I knew I couldn't afford to buy it and just sit on it, so we started doing this. At any point we have (farms that range) between 200 and 300 acres up to as many as 1,200 to 1,400 acres."

His only other business venture in retirement was owning an ad specialty and trophy business, a company he soon decided was too much work for the amount of return involved.

Much of his work since retiring has involved raising his five children, four girls and a boy, with the help of his wife, Jill. He says the only time he really feels his age is when he looks at the pictures of the kids as they have been growing up.

"It's really hard to believe it's been 23 or 24 years since I started playing baseball," Dayley said. "I don't really think it can be that long, but it's true. It just doesn't seem possible."

Where Have You Gone?

TOM LAWLESS

After eight years of managing in the minor leagues, from Cedar Rapids and Frederick to Peoria and Fort Wayne in between, Tom Lawless has not abandoned his dream, but he has become more of a realist.

Lawless's goal when he began managing in the minors was to work his way up to become a manager in the major leagues, or at least to be a major league coach, but he has started to wonder if that is ever going to happen.

"I've come to the conclusion that managing in the minor leagues has nothing to do with getting a job in the majors," Lawless said. "Eight years should be enough experience. I've proved what I can do."

Lawless, who will work again for the Baltimore Orioles in 2005, but as a roving instructor in the minor leagues teaching baserunning as well as working with infielders and outfielders, has been disappointed he has not been at least considered for a big-league coaching job.

"I've come close a couple of times," he said. "I thought I had a chance with Mike Hargrove in Seattle this year but it didn't happen. I'm surprised how the game has changed. It used to be that you paid your dues in the minor leagues and moved up. Now it's a matter of who you know.

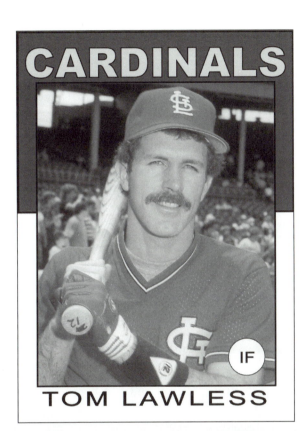

TOM LAWLESS
Seasons with Cardinals: 1985-1988

Best season with Cardinals: 1986

Games: 46 • At-bats: 39 • BA: .282 • 2B: 1 • RBI: 3 • R: 5 • SB: 8

"It used to be that if you did good in the minor leagues you moved up. Now nobody moves up—they just move around. I didn't think I would stay in the minor leagues forever, but that's the way it's happened."

Lawless doesn't want to sound bitter or depressed. He just understands the way the game is played now more than he did a few years ago.

"I've been around long enough now that I know several of the big league managers. But they don't hire coaches, the general managers do," Lawless said. "I know some of them, but there aren't any openings in those cities. Since Whitey (Herzog) left, I haven't had anybody who would give me a big league job.

"I am 47 years old, what else am I going to do? I enjoy what I do, so I keep on doing it. I've been able to take my family a lot of places because of baseball."

Lawless and his wife, Cheryl, are the parents of three girls—ages 21, 18 and 12—and he knows he is lucky because they all love baseball. The favorite place the family has been due to Lawless's work was the four months they spent in Australia when Lawless was managing a winter league team there a few years ago.

"I had to drag my family out of there," said Lawless, who lived about an hour north of Sydney. "They didn't want to leave. It was like the Miami Beach of Australia. When I win the lottery I am going to move there."

Lawless also has played and managed in Puerto Rico, but turned down a change to go work in Italy.

Lawless had plenty of time to study and learn baseball while playing in the major leagues, because he was on the bench a lot more often than on the field. His career lasted from 1982 through 1990, but he never played more than 59 games in a season. He was with the Cardinals from 1985 to 1988, and also played for Cincinnati, Montreal and Toronto. He was once traded, by the Reds to Montreal, to bring Pete Rose back to Cincinnati.

Lawless will forever be remembered by Cardinals fans for his unlikely and dramatic home run against the Twins in the 1987 World Series.

He started at third base in Game 4 of the series, at Busch Stadium, with the Cardinals trailing the Twins two games to one. The game was tied at 1 when the Cardinals came to bat in the fourth inning. Tony Pena led off the inning against Twins ace Frank Viola with a walk and Jose Oquendo followed with a single.

That brought Lawless, who hit only two home runs during 343 regular-season games in his career, to the plate. He responded with a three-run blast over the left field wall that ignited a six-run inning and carried the Cardinals to a 7-2 victory.

Almost as improbable as the homer was Lawless's bat flip, which took about as long to come down as it did for the ball to disappear over the fence.

Any other career highlight would surely not bear mention in the same breath when compared to his big hit against the Twins. But a couple others achieved while playing for the Toronto Blue Jays still stick out in Lawless's memory.

"The [World Series] home run tops my list," said Lawless, "but I always will remember standing on second base in Toronto and watching us pinch hit for the catcher. I knew we had already used all of our catchers, I was all that was left. I had to catch the ninth inning with a borrowed glove, borrowed shin guards, everything. Tom Henke was pitching and the first guy got on and tried to steal, and I threw him out.

"The other highlight came when [Mark] Langston was working on a no-hitter and beating us 1-0. Jimy Williams was managing and he pinch hit me for Lloyd Moseby. I thought he had lost his mind. But I got a hit, we scored two runs and won the game 2-1."

Lawless, who has managed in the Cardinals, Angels, Mets and Baltimore farm systems, has changed what he really wants out of the game because of his frustration.

"I want to be around people who are truthful and treat you fairly," Lawless said. "That's how I am trying to run my life in baseball. When kids ask me something, I tell them the truth. As a player I got lied to a couple of times and I am not going to do that. I want to be honest and upfront with kids. I have seen too many people in the game who are not truthful and it drives me crazy."

That's one of the reasons Lawless is so open about his desire to move up to the major leagues. He also needs three more years of major league service time to reach the 10-year level for calculating his pension.

"Maybe sometime I will catch a break," he said. "That's all I want."

KENT BOTTENFIELD

K ent Bottenfield has traded his baseball glove for a keyboard and microphone.

The former pitcher is performing these days as a Christian recording artist, having released his first CD, *Take Me Back*, in November 2004.

"I bought into a recording studio in Indianapolis that was doing some Christian projects, and it just seemed like a natural fit," Bottenfield said. "I had always been interested in music. I used to take my keyboard with me when we went on the road, but I realized my interests were being divided, so I pushed music aside until baseball was over."

The end of his career came in 2001, before he wanted it to, when Bottenfield realized he would not be able to return from a torn rotator cuff and a detached bicep tendon. He was 32 years old.

"I wanted to continue to play, but it was not going to happen," he said.

The transition away from baseball was difficult, but luckily for Bottenfield, his music career came along very soon after his baseball career ended.

"When you have played baseball for 16 years and had a schedule set for you it was a tough adjustment to make," he said. "It's been better than I thought it was going to be because you always see guys who can't ever figure out what it is they want to do.

Todd Warshaw/Getty Images

KENT BOTTENFIELD
Seasons with Cardinals: 1998-1999

Best season with Cardinals: 1999 (All-Star)

Games: 31 • Record: 18-7 (fourth in NL in wins) • **ERA: 3.97**
IP: 190.3 • **Hits: 197** • **SO: 124** • **BB: 89**

"I'm not the kind of guy who is just going to go out and play golf every day. I've got to have a purpose."

Bottenfield has found that with his singing career. He set up an 18-month plan for the expansion of the recording business, including the national release of his CD, and plans to bring out a second CD at the end of that period. He is trying to schedule concerts on the weekends, wrapped up by appearances in churches on Sunday, so he can spend time at home with his family during the week.

Bottenfield has moved his family—wife Pamela, daughter Emma, nine, son Eli, seven, and daughter Lucy, two—to a suburb of Indianapolis. Bottenfield and his wife had lived in Florida for 10 years but decided they did not want to raise their children there.

"I was born and raised in Oregon, so this was about halfway between Florida and Oregon," he said. "I had played here for a couple of years in Triple-A and we really got involved in a church here and liked the area.

"Part of me wishes the kids had been older so they could have seen me play, but it also is great to be here with them. It's nice to be done playing so I can be involved at this time in their lives.

Bottenfield played in a lot of places during his career, both in the minors and majors. He had stops in Montreal, Colorado, San Francisco and the Cubs before joining St. Louis in 1998. His best season in the majors came with the Cardinals in 1999, when he went 18-7 with a 3.97 ERA, posting career highs in victories, innings pitched, and strikeouts. For his efforts, Bottenfield was named an All-Star.

There was no indication Bottenfield was going to have such sudden success in St. Louis. After all, he had won no more than five games in a season before and had spent portions of several years pitching in the minors. He was also transitioning back into the starting rotation after several years of being used primarily in the bullpen.

In fact, his performance in his first season in St. Louis in 1998 was more typical of his career, as he won just four games, collected four saves, and bounced back and forth between the rotation and the pen.

His emergence the next season came at a time when the Cardinals were desperately searching for pitching help, and he provided it with his 18 victories, double the total of Darren Oliver, who finished the season second on the team in wins. He expected to continue to pitch that well in 2000 for the Cardinals, until he received the news late in spring training that he had been traded.

Bottenfield was upset by the trade that sent him to the Angels, as were many Cardinals fans. But his legacy has continued for years to come—even after his playing career was over—because he was the bait used to lure centerfielder Jim Edmonds from California. Edmonds has gone on to post one spectacular season after another for St. Louis.

Unfortunately for Bottenfield, he was not able to continue the success he found in 1999. He won seven games for the Angels before he was traded late in the 2000 season to the Phillies. He then finished up with the Astros in 2001 while trying to come back from his injury. He never matched the success he had in one season in St. Louis, winning a combined 18 games the rest of his major league career.

All that has become history now, as Bottenfield settled into his new career. He was surprised at some of the similarities between baseball and the recording business, citing the attention to detail and the long hours involved, both in practice and performances, if one wants to become successful.

"It is extremely detailed and very tedious (work)," Bottenfield said of the music business. "You spend lots and lots of hours going over songs. You are singing the songs in your sleep because you go over them so much."

Bottenfield actually writes the words and the music and does the vocals for many of the songs.

"I love the creative process," he said. "I always thought I would be involved in music when I was done with baseball, I just didn't know for sure what I would be doing."

A chance meeting in a Milwaukee hotel lobby late in the 2004 season led to another job for Bottenfield—preparing scouting reports for the pitchers on the teams the Cardinals were projected to play in the playoffs.

"I was in Milwaukee promoting the CD and the Cardinals were there and I was at the hotel to meet some friends," Bottenfield said. "Tony (La Russa) saw me and it looked like he had seen a ghost. He said, 'We were just talking about you this morning.'"

La Russa wanted to know if Bottenfield had any interest or desire to take on the part-time scouting assignment, which actually called for him to review tapes of each of the pitchers the Cardinals might face in the playoffs. Bottenfield had been involved in using video of hitters to prepare for his games as a pitcher, and the Cardinals thought he could use the same approach for analyzing opposing pitchers.

Bottenfield agreed to do it, and scouted the Dodgers and Giants, whom the Cardinals thought they might face in the first round, breaking down through video each of the pitchers' strengths and weaknesses.

Bottenfield enjoyed the experience, and there is a chance he will be doing similar projects for the Cardinals in the future.

He won't, however, become a full-time scout, traveling the country while observing different players. He personally believes that kind of scouting is becoming outdated because of the ability of video.

"You can see more on the video, and you can save all of the money for not having to travel every place," he said. "I think this is the way of the future."

How much of his future is devoted to scouting by video might be determined by how successful his music career becomes.

"We're going to spend a few months promoting the first CD, then come back in and start writing and then recording the second CD," Bottenfield said. "It is a lot of fun."

Where Have You Gone?

RICK WISE

It turned out to be a lot easier for Rick Wise to make the major leagues as a pitcher than as a coach.

Wise was a "bonus baby" when he signed with the Philadelphia Phillies after high school in 1964, before the annual amateur draft was instituted. Because of the amount of the signing bonus he received, he had to stay on the major league roster for a year before he could be sent to the minors. Wise spent that season in Philadelphia as an 18-year-old, going 5-3 in 25 games, mostly in relief.

After spending 1965 in Triple-A, Wise was back in the major leagues in 1966 and stayed there for the next 15 seasons, retiring early in 1982. After taking a couple of years off, Wise began coaching in the minor leagues in 1985 with the expectation that after a few years, he would have the chance to become a pitching coach in the majors.

Fifteen years later, he gave up on that ever becoming a reality.

"I was really disappointed that I never got the chance to work on the major league level," Wise said. "What I found is there are a lot of politics involved in baseball. I just got tired and frustrated by it."

Despite working for the Boston, Oakland and Houston organizations, Wise said he was never seriously considered for a major league job, and saw people with less experience and fewer credentials continue to pass by him and receive those opportunities.

ST. LOUIS CARDINALS

RICK
WISE   PITCHER

RICK WISE
Seasons with Cardinals: 1972-1973

Best season with Cardinals: 1973 (All-Star)

Games: 35 • Record: 16-12 (seventh in NL in wins) • **ERA: 3.37**
IP: 259 (eighth in NL) • **Hits: 259** • SO: 144 • **BB: 59**
CG: 14 (fourth in NL) • **SHO: 5 (third in NL)**

"I saw other fellows who had not been around as long as I had or who had not had the success I had getting shots in the major leagues, and that frustrates you," he said.

Still, Wise could not think of any other job he would rather be doing, so he has spent the last five years working as a pitching coach in the independent Atlantic League. For the past two seasons, he's been working in Nashua, New Hampshire. He will be returning to the league in 2005 to work with former Cardinal Tom Herr, who will manage the new Lancaster, Pennsylvania, franchise in the league.

"I like having the winters free to travel and re-connect with my family," said Wise, who has lived in the Portland, Oregon, area for the last 25 years. "We have two kids and four grandchildren all within about a 20- or 25-mile area."

Wise spent only two of his 16 major-league seasons in St. Louis, but is a famous person in the franchise's history. He was the player acquired by the Cardinals in spring training 1972 when owner Gussie Busch ordered general manager Bing Devine to trade Steve Carlton because of a salary dispute.

At the time it was viewed as a fairly even trade. Wise was only 26 years old and had been pitching in the majors for seven years; but nobody knew Carlton would go on to win 300 games and become a Hall of Famer.

Wise was a good pitcher in his two seasons in St. Louis. He won 16 games each year, with ERAs a shade over three runs a game, and was actually the starting pitcher in the 1973 All-Star game. In 1972, he was involved in 19 one-run games, and lost 12 of them.

Carlton's St. Louis teammates at the time were not as upset about the trade as history might suggest they should have been.

"I thought we were getting a good pitcher who could help us," first baseman Joe Torre said. "We knew Carlton was a good pitcher too, but he and Mr. Busch had reached an impasse. It happened at a bad time because it was right before the strike, and Mr. Busch took it very personal. We were probably treated better than any other club, and it hurt him very deeply and he reacted to it. He made up his mind and that was that."

Even though Devine had been ordered by Busch to trade Carlton, he did not consider it to be a lopsided deal.

"Both are capable, winning and productive pitchers," Devine said at the time. "One is left-handed, one is right-handed."

Wise said he never considered it a negative slap against him that he was traded for Carlton.

"Carlton and I are good friends," said Wise, who was involved in a contract dispute with the Phillies at the same time Carlton was battling the Cardinals, which made the trade possible. "We go hunting in the winter together. The trade surprised me, because I thought we would get it worked out."

Later in his career, he was traded again, by Boston to Cleveland, for another pitcher who made the Hall of Fame, Dennis Eckersley.

The Cardinals had traded Wise, along with Bernie Carbo, to Boston after the 1973 season for Reggie Smith and Ken Tatum. That trade disappointed him, because he had moved to the St. Louis area and planned to continue to live there. He actually kept his home in St. Louis through 1979, when he decided to move back to his native Oregon. He finished his playing career with two seasons with the Indians and then two years in San Diego.

Wise will celebrate his 60th birthday in 2005, but has no plans to alter his schedule of coaching in the summer.

"I've dedicated my life to baseball and have poured my life into it," he said. "It is something I look forward to every spring. As long as I stay healthy and keep enjoying it as much as I do I intend to keep going."

Where Have You Gone?

STEVE BRAUN

As he was nearing the end of his 15-year playing career in the major leagues, Steve Braun began to think about what he would do with the rest of his life. He wasn't certain how it would happen, but he thought he would somehow remain in baseball.

His opportunity came in 1986, when he was finishing as a player at the Cardinals' Triple A Louisville club. Jim Fregosi was managing the club and left in mid-season to become the manager of the Chicago White Sox. Mike Jorgensen was switched from a roving hitting instructor in the Cardinals' system to the manager at Louisville, creating an opening for a hitting instructor.

Braun did not have to think twice about taking the job. Nineteen years later, he is still coaching.

As is usually the case in minor league baseball, Braun has moved around during his coaching career, which has included only one season, 1990, at the major league level, working as the hitting coach for the Cardinals under Whitey Herzog.

For a dozen years, Braun worked for the Boston Red Sox, including eight seasons as the organization's hitting coordinator. For the past two years, he has been the coach for the Yankees' Double A team in Trenton, New Jersey, in the Eastern League. That has been a convenient job for Braun considering that Trenton is his hometown, and that for three of the four seasons prior to 2003, he was a coach there when the franchise was the Double A affiliate of the Red Sox.

CARDINALS OUTFIELD
STEVE BRAUN

STEVE BRAUN
Seasons with Cardinals: 1981-1985

Best season with Cardinals: 1983

Games: 78 • At-bats: 92 • BA: .272 • OBP: .404
SLG: .413 • HR: 3 • RBI: 7 • R: 8

"I really enjoy the Double A level," said the 57-year-old Braun. "You see a lot of good players come through this league. We've also had some players with major league experience who come back to this league to try to work their way back to the majors."

Like any minor league coach or manager, Braun knows his job is to help develop the players and get them ready for the major leagues. That left him with a bit of a dilemma during the 2004 playoffs and World Series. During his many years with the Red Sox, he had worked with hitters such as Trot Nixon and Jason Varitek, and he wished them success in the playoffs. But since he was now working for the Yankees, he could not cheer too loudly for them. Then, when the Red Sox came back to beat the Yankees and reach the World Series, they found the Cardinals, Braun's old team, waiting for them.

Braun's major league career began with the Minnesota Twins in 1971, but even though he played regularly for them for several years and also played for Seattle, Kansas City and Toronto before joining the Cardinals in 1981, some of his most favorite memories of his career came in St. Louis.

Braun was used almost exclusively as a pinch-hitter during his five years in St. Louis, and he excelled at the job. His 60 career pinch-hits ranks him second in the all-time Cardinals' record book.

"I always tell people the years I spent in St. Louis was when I had the most fun in baseball," Braun said. "I can remember getting great ovations when I led off the ninth inning as a pinch-hitter and drew a walk. That's how into the game everybody was there.

"The only chance I had to be on a World Champion came in St. Louis in 1982 and I was there in 1985 as well. I had the best seat in the house and I didn't have to pay for it."

He has to admit, however, that he found himself cheering more for the Red Sox than the Cardinals during the 2004 World Series.

"The fans of Boston had been so faithful and I knew working as a Red Sox instructor that you really approached the job and each season with that goal (winning the World Series, and doing it for the fans) in mind," he said. "It really is something you think about."

So when some of "his" players did well, Braun was happy, just as he has been happy in the past with other players that he believes he has helped on their way to the majors, a group that included Todd

Zeile, Ray Lankford and Bernard Gilkey when he was a Cardinals' coach.

"I enjoy helping the young players because I know they have the same dream that I had when I was a young player, the dream of getting to the major leagues," Braun said. "The kids today are bigger and stronger than when I played, but I think the game has stayed the same. I still try to teach the fundamentals, and strike zone discipline, because I think if they learn that then the power will come if it is meant to be."

Braun is under contract to the Yankees through the 2005 season, but he still does not know what his specific coaching assignment will be for the season, although he expects to be someplace other than Trenton. He knows that being in the same place for five of the last six seasons in the minors is a real rarity anyway.

Braun also has been running camps and clinics for youth players in the Trenton area, and he will perhaps begin doing that on a more regular basis if he decides not to return to a minor league job in 2006. He also hopes to spend more time with his first grandchild, who lives with Braun's daughter in Minnesota. Braun also has an adult son who lives in Trenton.

"I just bought a home here in 2004 so I have plans to stay here," Braun says. "I play a lot of golf, and would like to get involved in more of the local over-50 amateur tournaments. I haven't lost my desire to compete, and that is a good outlet for me."

VINCE COLEMAN

W hen Vince Coleman reached first base, he could feel and hear the electricity that flowed through the crowd at Busch Stadium in anticipation of one thing: a stolen base.

"Somebody used to say that they shut down the concession stands whenever I got on base," Coleman said. "That was my biggest thrill in a Cardinal uniform, getting on base and hearing the crowd."

The art of the stolen base has been lost for the most part in major league baseball these days, with the game so focused on home runs. Coleman believes that is a mistake, and he is doing his part to try to keep the stolen base and the importance of good baserunning alive.

In the fall of 2003, he was having dinner with former teammate Terry Pendleton, now a coach for the Braves, when the Braves were playing the Diamondbacks in Phoenix, where Coleman lives. Pendleton asked him if he had any interest in becoming a coach. That conversation led Pendleton to discuss the matter with Atlanta general manager John Schuerholz, who proceeded to offer Coleman a job working in the team's fall instructional league in Florida.

"I wanted to see if I liked it," Coleman said. "It turned out I loved it. I loved working with the young kids, giving them instruction. They seemed to respond pretty well to what I said. I was just providing basic concepts, the things a runner should look for when they get on base."

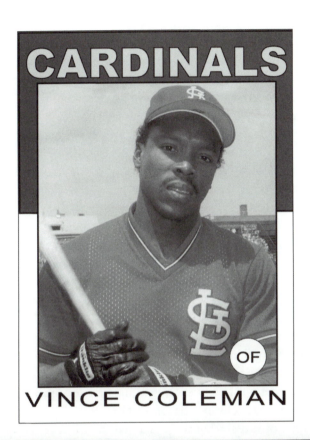

VINCE COLEMAN
Seasons with Cardinals: 1985-1990

Best season with Cardinals: 1987

Games: 151 • At-Bats: 623 (third in NL) • BA: .289 • OBP: .363
H: 180 (fourth in NL) • 3B: 10 (fifth in NL) • HR: 3 • RBI: 43
R: 121 (second in NL) • SB: 109 (first in NL)

Coleman knows more than most about what makes a smart baserunner tick. After all, he led the National League in stolen bases all six seasons he was with the Cardinals, averaging 91.5 steals per season over that span.

"All of their lives kids are told how not to run the bases," Coleman said. "'Don't get picked off. Don't get too big a lead. Don't get thrown out going from first to third. Don't make the first or last out at third base.' Because of that they run defensively. I was telling them how to run offensively, giving them tips and things to look for from the pitcher that would give them an advantage."

Cubs' manager Dusty Baker found out what Coleman was doing and called to offer him a similar job, working throughout the season in the Cubs' system. When Coleman found out the Cardinals were not interested in his services, Coleman went to work for the Cubs in spring training 2004.

"I work in spring training, which is great because I get to stay at home, and then I make my own schedule during the season. I spend 15 days each month going to the different minor league clubs and I also work with the major league team. I am home for 10 days every month."

The flexibility of making his own schedule was important for Coleman. Since he moved to Arizona, he has become an avid golfer. He competes regularly on the Celebrity Players Tour with several other former Cardinals and former major leaguers.

Coleman met with great success in his first season with the Cubs. Two of his projects, Dwaine Bacon of Double A West Tennessee and Chris Walker of Class A Lansing, each led their league with 60 stolen bases.

Coleman, 43, gets upset when he sees the lack of emphasis on the stolen base in today's game because it was such a critical component of the Runnin' Redbirds' success in the 1980s. He stole 110 bases as a rookie and followed that season with stolen base totals of 107, 109, 81, 65 and 77. His speed, and that of his teammates, kept the pressure on the opponents and forced them into many mistakes.

He knows the game is different now, but he still maintains players should be stealing more bases.

"There are people hitting .230 and they can't run," Coleman said. "I could leg out .250 even today. People say you can't steal bases today because all of the pitchers use the slide step. There are still ways to steal. A pitcher always gives off tips before he starts his delivery to the plate. You have to study film and read the pitcher.

"I learned it from Don Blasingame when I was in the minors with the Cardinals. There is homework you have to do to be successful. It's not just pure speed."

During Coleman's day, the Cardinals had a camera in their dugout near first base which focused on the opposing pitcher. If Coleman or the other runners were having a difficult time figuring out his move to first, they would go in the video room and watch the tape during the game. That was one of the advantages to having the home team dugout along the first base line, Coleman said.

"Not many people knew about it, but we used it all the time," he said.

If Coleman has any regrets about his career, it was that he chose to accept a higher contract and leave St. Louis after the 1990 season as a free agent, signing with the Mets.

The move was not based entirely on money, but a desire to win, Coleman said. He thought the Cardinals had lost so many players through free agency, and that the Mets, especially with their deeper starting rotation, had a greater chance to be successful. It didn't work out that way, of course, and when Coleman struggled with the Mets and got involved in some off-field troubles, he was vilified by the New York media.

"I was used to winning," Coleman said. "Going to the World Series was the only thing I could relate to. I thought the Mets would win. It didn't happen. I got hurt, other guys got hurt and we finished last. Nothing worked out. It snowballed into a bad apple, and I didn't recover from it.

"I was getting ripped in the papers every day, and because I was the highest paid player on the team, when we didn't win it was my fault."

Coleman spent three unhappy years in New York before he was traded to Kansas City in 1994. He finished his career by bouncing from the Royals, to Seattle, to Cincinnati and to Detroit, retiring in

1997. Coleman finished his career with 752 stolen bases, but never stole more than 50 in a season after leaving St. Louis.

Life these days is good for Coleman, who moved to the Phoenix area in 1988 out of his friendship with former football Cardinals' receiver Roy Green and his desire to play golf every day in the winter. His two sons, Vincent and Lance, are in high school. Vincent, a 16-year-old junior, is developing into a good football prospect, scoring 10 touchdowns as a running back this season. Lance is a 15-year-old sophomore and was the team's kicker this year. Both boys also play baseball.

Coleman also re-married in November 2004 and spent part of his winter traveling to the Bahamas to participate in Michael Jordan's golf tournament and to the Dominican Republic, where he helped run a week-long youth baseball clinic.

"I knew when I got out of baseball raising my two boys was going to be my full-time job, and I have been fortunate to be around them every day as they are growing up. Now that they are in high school I don't have to coach them every day, and I can move on to some other things I want to do.

"They say you should do what you know best, and for me that is talking about stealing bases and running the bases, and with the Cubs I have somebody that wants me to do that. Things could not be any better."

Where Have You Gone?

BUD SMITH

It isn't often that a 21-year-old pitcher throws a no-hitter in the major leagues, and afterward basically disappears. Yet, that is pretty much what has happened to Bud Smith.

On September 3, 2001, a month before his 22nd birthday, Smith threw a no-hitter for the Cardinals against the San Diego Padres. It was only the ninth no-hitter in the 109 years the Cardinals had been playing in the National League.

The left-handed Smith walked four and struck out seven in the 4-0 victory. It was only the fourth win of his major league career. His most challenging moment of the game came when future Hall of Famer Tony Gwynn came off the bench to pinch hit.

"Since he wasn't in the starting lineup we had not gone over him," Smith said. "It was the first time I had ever faced him. I grew up in southern California and went to his camps. It was his last year but he was still hitting .330 or something. I remember thinking, 'He hits everything.' I decided to try to get ahead in the count with a fastball and not try to do too much. On the second pitch he hit a line drive one-hopper to short and (Edgar) Renteria made the play and threw him out. He hit it right on the nose, but we were playing him up the middle.

"Warming up for the game I didn't really feel any different (than usual). I just remember being really focused during the game because I had faced them in my previous start in St. Louis and they had hit me pretty good. I don't know if they took me lightly or what, because

Elsa/Getty Images

BUD SMITH
P
ST. LOUIS CARDINALS

BUD SMITH
Seasons with Cardinals: 2001-2002

Best season with Cardinals: 2001

Games: 16 • Record: **6-3** • **ERA: 3.83** • IP: 84.7
Hits: 79 • SO: **59** • **CG: 1** • SHO: 1

I knew after the first time through the lineup they really had not had any tough at-bats. Then I could tell about the sixth or seventh inning that they were starting to press. By that point I was really locked into the game. Our defense made some good plays."

Heading into the 2005 season, Smith has followed up that no-hitter with only three additional major league victories, two that season and one in 2002. His other career highlight was pitching five innings of four-hit, one-run ball to help the Cardinals avoid elimination in Game 4 of the 2001 Division Series against Arizona. The Diamondbacks did eliminate the Cardinals the following day.

Ever since that moment, however, Smith seems to have been battling arm injuries and tough luck. He left the Cardinals in July 2002 when he, Mike Timlin and Placido Polanco were traded to the Phillies for Scott Rolen.

"At first I was disappointed," Smith said. "I thought my first year wasn't bad, and I was struggling a bit in 2002 with some arm problems and when I heard my name in trade talks I wondered why they would want to trade me. When I found out they were getting Scott Rolen I couldn't blame them."

Smith went to the Phillies with a positive attitude. He reported to Triple-A Scranton expecting to make a few starts, then move back up to the major leagues. In his third start at Scranton, however, he tore the labrum in his pitching arm and had to undergo surgery.

He went through a winter of rehab and was ready to throw in spring training but not under game conditions. He was assigned to Double-A to continue his rehab. His arm was feeling good, but Smith found out that was a false hope. He came back too soon and tore the labrum again, in a different spot.

A second operation followed, and Smith began to wonder if a baseball career was meant to be. He received encouragement by the fact that he was still young, and the knowledge that there were pitchers in the major leagues who had had four or five arm operations.

Another rehab stint followed, and when he reported to spring training in 2004, the Phillies said they were going to make him a reliever. He worked in spring training, then was assigned to Triple-A to open the season. After making his final Florida appearance in 90-

degree weather, he made his first regular season start in Canada, where he said the temperature felt like seven degrees.

"I threw three innings, but I couldn't get loose," Smith said. "I woke up the next day and I couldn't lift my arm above my shoulder. Everything was inflamed."

That meant another two months on the disabled list, which basically signaled the end of his career with the Phillies. When he came back, they assigned him to Clearwater in the Class-A Florida State League and he finished the 2004 season there.

"I can't say too many good things about the Philadelphia organization," Smith said. "They paid for two surgeries. They were not too happy with me that I got hurt again last year, because they had some injuries on the big league level and needed guys to come up and pitch and I was hurt. They basically were giving me a slap in the face by sending me to A ball and keeping me there. Ever since I got [to Philadelphia] my arm just kind of fell apart."

Smith, who still lives in the Long Beach area, is optimistic about the 2005 season and his future, however. He has signed a minor-league contract with the Minnesota Twins and believes the fresh start in a new organization will be good for him.

The Twins have said their intention is for him to work as a reliever, start the year in Triple-A and maybe be ready to pitch in the big leagues by the middle of the season.

"I've been throwing and staying in shape," he said. "I think with the arm problems I have pitching out of the bullpen may be better for me than trying to throw 100 pitches every five days.

"With everything I have, gone through, I am still only 25 years old. I know that when I was 21 I was able to get guys out in the big leagues. I knew how to throw then, but I didn't really know how to pitch. Now I have so much more knowledge about pitching. I can't throw 86-88 mph like I did before the surgeries, but I still should throw 84-85. I just have to keep learning from the guys around me and get smarter about how to pitch.

"I think I am in a better organization that will give me a chance to get healthy and work my way back to the big leagues. That's what I want to do."

Where Have You Gone?

JEFF LAHTI

Jeff Lahti took his winning share from the 1982 World Series and used it to buy a 90-acre farm in the Columbia River Gorge in Oregon, about an hour east of Portland. The farm resides nearby the area where he grew up.

Twenty-two years later he is still there, living in a house he had built in the middle of what is now a thriving orchard full of apple and pear trees.

"All these years I've been waiting for it to start coming around and now it is finally happening," Lahti said. "We had only a five-acre clump of trees when we bought it, but we planted the trees on the rest of the property and now they are starting to get old enough to produce. They should be producing for the rest of my life."

Lahti has even expanded his property by adding another 60 acres to his orchard, bringing his total to about 8,000 trees. He named the farm All-Star Acres during a New Year's Eve party in 1983. This year's crop should fill about 2,000 four foot-by-four foot bins, which he takes and sells to a warehouse in Yakima, Washington.

"That was always my plan, to buy a farm after I got out of baseball," Lahti said. "I have wondered at times why I did it, but hopefully it is coming around."

Lahti's plan for his baseball career did not work out as he had hoped. He was limited to just four years in the major leagues with the

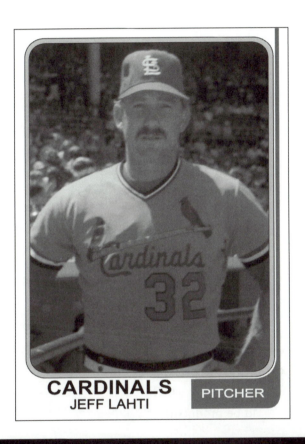

CARDINALS
JEFF LAHTI
PITCHER

JEFF LAHTI
Seasons with Cardinals: 1982-1986

Best season with Cardinals: 1985

Games: 52 • Record: 5-2 • SV: 19 (seventh in NL) • ERA: 1.84
IP: 68.3 • Hits: 63 • SO: 41

Cardinals between 1982 and 1986 after a torn rotator cuff ended his career at the age of 30.

"It was way too short," he said. "I had three good seasons, and we went to the World Series twice. Some people play 20 years and never get there. I tried to come back after the surgery, but I found I could only pitch about once every six days.

"I can't complain about where baseball took me. It was short lived, but it was great fun while it lasted. Without baseball I wouldn't have what I am looking at right now, or I would have had to work a lot harder to get it."

Lahti's home, which he built in 1986, is at the end of a mile-long driveway off a two-lane country road. His home sits on a hill overlooking the river valley below.

"It's pretty peaceful," he said. "It's kind of removed from the world a little bit. We don't get a lot of baseball games on television."

Lahti gets his baseball fix by working as the head coach at Hood River High School, a school of about 1,200 kids. He took over a struggling program in 2003 that won only five games over a combined four seasons. Last year, Lahti took the team to within one out of winning a spot in the state playoffs.

"It was pretty exciting," he said. "We had a one-run lead with one out to go in the game and they hit a popup behind second base. It was a tough play and it hit off our second baseman's hand. The tying run scored and they won the game in the next inning, 7-6.

"We had 11 seniors, so we are pretty much starting over this year. We have a couple of good pitchers coming, so I think we will be pretty competitive."

Lahti relies a great deal on his baseball experiences and memories in his coaching. "I always have a story for them," he said. He no doubt tells them about his one appearance as a starting pitcher in 1982, when manager Whitey Herzog made the mistake of telling Lahti a couple of days ahead of time that he was going to start. The already-hyper Lahti was even more animated than usual prior to his start, arriving at Riverfront Stadium in Cincinnati about eight hours before the game was supposed to start.

"[Whitey] told me way too early," Lahti said, and Herzog vowed never to make that mistake again.

Lahti had joined the Cardinals just before opening day in 1982 in a trade with Jose Brito from Cincinnati for pitcher Bob Shirley. He had been drafted and signed by the Reds in 1978 after rejecting offers from the Phillies in the 1976 draft and the Giants in the 1977 draft.

Lahti's best season for the Cardinals was 1985, when he led the team with 19 saves and worked as the closer until Todd Worrell was called up from Triple A Louisville in August. When Bruce Sutter signed with the Braves as a free agent after the 1984 season, the Cardinals were left with a bullpen-by-committee, an arrangement which allowed Lahti to pick up most of the save opportunities early in the 1985 season. He was one of the relievers juggled by Herzog, who mixed and matched situations where he thought Lahti, Rick Horton, Ken Dayley and others had the greatest chance to be successful.

It worked well for Lahti, who in addition to recording 19 of his 20 career saves, posted a 5-2 record with a 1.84 ERA. He likely would have continued as an effective middle reliever for several years if not for his career-ending injury. He only pitched in four games after that season, all in April 1986, because of his shoulder injury.

His career highlights include the famous Game 5 of the 1985 NLCS against the Dodgers, when Ozzie Smith's home run made him the winning pitcher.

"I can still throw batting practice, but if I try to throw too hard then I can't move my arm," he said. "Twenty years later, the pain is still there."

In addition to running the orchard and coaching the high school team, Lahti has been involved in several business ventures over the years, including a stint as a distributor for Anheuser-Busch that did not work out.

Lahti has two daughters from his first marriage, and they live with their mother in Cleveland. He has remarried, and he and his second wife, Deane, have a daughter, Rachel, who is eight. He has two stepchildren who are away from home, one in college and the other in the military.

He doesn't wander too far from home these days because of all the work that has to be done on his farm. That makes keeping up with many of his former teammates, who have remained in St. Louis, a difficult task.

"Once growing season starts you have to keep up with it," he said. "There is a science to being a farmer. It is not an easy job."

Where Have You Gone?

TED SIMMONS

T ed Simmons knows exactly when his world changed—June 8, 1993.

Simmons was in his office, working as the general manager of the Pittsburgh Pirates, when he felt pain in his upper left arm. He also was suffering from cramps. Ninety minutes later, he was in surgery. Simmons had suffered a heart attack.

"Luckily I was able to recognize the symptoms, and smart enough to get myself to a hospital," Simmons said. "An artery was blocked, and I underwent an angioplasty."

As he came out of the hospital, and began his recovery, Simmons made a major career decision. Eleven days after suffering the heart attack, Simmons resigned as the GM of the Pirates.

"It changed my whole perspective on life," Simmons said of the heart attack. "I was 44 years old. Generally when that happens to you at that age you are dead by the time you are 50 unless you make some changes in your lifestyle. You can continue not exercising, smoking and eating unhealthy, but I decided I wanted to live."

Simmons is now 55 years old and tremendously enjoying life, as well as his new job working for the San Diego Padres.

"This is the best thing I could be doing," Simmons said.

Simmons made the decision that he wanted to stay in baseball after his playing career, but not in uniform, away from managing or coaching. When he retired from the Atlanta Braves after the 1988

ST. LOUIS CARDINALS

TED SIMMONS   CATCHER

TED SIMMONS
Seasons with Cardinals: 1968-1980

Best season with Cardinals: 1975 (sixth in NL MVP voting)

Games: 157 • At-bats: 581 • Hits: 193 (fourth in NL)
BA: .332 (second in NL) • OBP: .396 (eighth in NL)
SLG: .491 (tenth in NL) • 2B: 32 • HR: 18 • RBI: 100 (eighth in NL)
R: 80 • Total bases: 285 (sixth in NL) • Int'l walks: 16 (third in NL)

season, he was hired by the Cardinals as their director of player development.

"I wanted a different kind of a challenge, because I had been in a uniform all my life," Simmons said. "Being a farm director is the most difficult job in baseball. At the time the Cardinals had eight farm teams, so in effect I was running eight teams at the same time. It ought to be a prerequisite to becoming a general manager, because if you can run five or six teams, which most clubs have now, you ought to be able to run one. The only difference is the number of zeroes."

Simmons was lured away from the Cardinals to become the Pirates' GM by Mark Sauer, who had left the Cardinals to become president of the Pirates. When he got to Pittsburgh, however, he knew his job would be different than the traditional general manager duties.

"Pittsburgh was about to lose the franchise," Simmons said. "There was a race going on about who would get to Tampa Bay first. The Giants were threatening to move there, and there was talk the Pirates might be going there too. Running the Pirates then was like a case in crisis management and it took its toll on me."

As he went through his medical rehab, however, Simmons knew he could not walk away from the game. He had become good friends with John Hart, then the general manager of the Cleveland Indians, and he was able to go to work a few months later as a major league scout for the Indians.

Simmons spent six years working for Cleveland before leaving to join Kevin Towers, the general manager in San Diego. His first job there was to overhaul the entire scouting and minor league departments, a task that took close to three years to complete.

Now that he has left those departments to others to run, Simmons is back working directly as an assistant to Towers, scouting all major league players and helping make evaluations for trades and free agent signings.

"What I do is help Kevin Towers decide who to pay and who not to pay," Simmons said.

That seemingly simple job description has become harder over the years, primarily because of the amount of money involved, and those decisions are not something Simmons takes lightly. He also has seen a change over the years in how those decisions are made, with many teams now relying as much on statistical analysis as they do on the personal recommendations of scouts.

"You have to be able to understand and appreciate both if you want to be successful today," said Simmons. "People who don't understand both or rely on both are going to be left behind, because the money involved has become so great."

Simmons has his own ideas about determining which players are worthy of signing to multiyear, multimillion dollar contracts.

"None of us are worth the money," Simmons said. "Babe Ruth was not worth the money. I was not worth the money. You have to make tough decisions and evaluations. You have to rely on your own history, of watching similar players and seeing whether or not they were successful. Sometimes you make the right decision and sometimes you are wrong. You need to be right most of the time."

The history that Simmons relies on mostly is a player's health. He is a lot more apt to spend money on a player who has consistently been in the lineup than a player who has frequent trips to the disabled list on his transactions page.

"History is history," Simmons said. "The sabermetrics guys can say they don't want to spend money on a player because he has too low of an OPS, but I can look at a player and say the only way I can feel good about paying the money is to give it to a player who you know is going to be playing every day."

The Cardinals made the right decision when they took Simmons out of the University of Michigan with their first-round pick in the 1967 draft. He made his major league debut the following year, and was the team's catcher through 1980. He was traded to Milwaukee before the 1981 season, and played there until joining the Braves in 1986 for the final three years of his career.

Whitey Herzog always maintained that if the National League had employed the designated hitter, he would never have traded Simmons to the Brewers. He toyed with the idea of moving Keith Hernandez to left field and playing Simmons at first base after signing Darrell Porter to be the Cardinals catcher, but Simmons was not in favor of that move.

Simmons never received the national attention he likely deserved while with the Cardinals, even though he was an six-time All-Star, hit .300 or better six seasons, topped 20 homers on five occasions and twice drove in more than 100 runs. He was forever playing in the shadow of the Reds' Johnny Bench, which kept him from earning more recognition.

Bench also was earning rave reviews as the catcher on the Big Red Machine, which logged a lot of postseason appearances. Simmons never played in a postseason game while a member of the Cardinals.

Still, in a 15-year span from 1971 through 1985, Simmons played at least 123 games 14 times. The only exception was the strike year of 1981. Eight times he played in 150 or more games, a remarkable show of endurance for a position player who racked up most of his starts as a catcher.

Over his career, he slugged 248 homers, drove in 1,389 runs and had a lifetime average of .285. Many observers believe he should have received much stronger consideration for the Hall of Fame.

That's a subject Simmons is reluctant to talk about, but he does appreciate being able to talk about baseball, or anything else, when he knows he could very easily have died years ago.

He won't totally eliminate the possibility of becoming a general manager again some day, but he is very comfortable working for the Padres and Towers, who have allowed him to maintain his home in St. Louis.

"I have the freedom to go and do what I need to do," Simmons said. "I am very involved, and I like that."

RON TAYLOR

While he was playing in the major leagues in the 1960s, Ron Taylor made several trips to Southeast Asia to visit U.S. troops fighting in the Vietnam War. On one of those visits, shortly after the Tet offensive, he was touring hospitals when it became clear to him what he wanted to do when his playing career was over.

Despite having a degree in electrical engineering, and a job working in that field during the winters, Taylor decided he wanted to go to medical school and become a doctor.

"I don't know of anybody else who decided to begin medical school after their career was over," Taylor said. "The only other doctors I know who played in the majors were already in school for that before and during their careers, Doc Medich and Bobby Brown."

For Taylor, the transformation from pitcher to doctor wasn't an easy one. Taylor was 34 years old when his 10-year career ended in 1972, and when he sat down with the dean of the medical school at the University of Toronto, in his hometown, he was told the school did not accept many older students.

"If I was 24 instead of 34 I would have been fine," Taylor said. "The dean was impressed by my academic record, however, and he told me that if I took a year of honors science classes and if I earned the same grades in those classes as I had in my engineering classes, they would consider my application.

RON TAYLOR
Seasons with Cardinals: 1963-1965

Best season with Cardinals: 1963

Games: 54 • Record: 9-7 • SV: 11 (seventh in NL) • ERA: 2.84
IP: 133.3 • Hits: 119 • SO: 91

"I hadn't been in school for 11 years, but that was what I did. I took chemistry, biology, all of those kinds of classes. The dean had told me whether I would be accepted or not depended on the personality of the admissions committee, and that I would probably have about a 50-50 chance of being accepted. I thought those were good enough odds, so I applied and was accepted."

Taylor was 35 years old when he entered medical school, completed his classes at the age of 39 and was 41 when he finished his residency and internship and set up his own private practice. If he had wanted to become a surgeon or another specialized doctor it would have required even more years of schooling, so he became a general practitioner.

"I think it better fits my personality, too," he said. "I think I have a pretty good understanding of problem solving."

Taylor has been running that general practice and a sports injury clinic in Toronto ever since. In addition, since the third year of the Blue Jays' existence, 1979, Taylor has been the team doctor for the ballclub.

"There's no question it changed my life," Taylor said of becoming a doctor. "I don't think I could be any happier doing anything else."

Taylor even threw batting practice for the Blue Jays for several years, but now at 67 years old, he has given up that assignment.

For almost all of his patients, he is known as Dr. Taylor, and there is no connection with his past life as a major league pitcher for the Indians, Cardinals, Astros, Mets and Padres. He has no pictures of himself as a player on the walls of his office, and he does not wear his World Series rings from the 1964 Cardinals, the 1969 Mets or either of the rings he earned as the Blue Jays' doctor when the team won the World Series in 1992 and 1993.

"I like it to be more of a curiosity and not a focus," Taylor said. "I would guess less than half of my patients know that I played baseball, and that number is only higher because there were some stories about me in the newspapers here during the playoffs in 2004.

"I want my patients to see me as a physician, not as a washed up baseball player."

Taylor said the highlights of his baseball career came during the 1964 World Series, particularly in Game 4, when the Cardinals trailed the Yankees two games to one. Playing at Yankee Stadium, the Cardinals fell behind 3-0 in the game and were in danger of going down three games to one before Ken Boyer hit a grand slam to salvage the game. Taylor then relieved and preserved the 4-3 victory by holding the Yankees hitless for the last four innings. The Cardinals went on to win the series in seven games.

He also won and saved a game in the 1969 NL playoffs for the Mets, and saved their first win in the World Series.

Taylor does have all of his baseball memorabilia in a room in his home where he retreats to watch football games on television and relax.

There might be another Taylor pitching in the major leagues some day, too, Taylor said. His oldest son, Drew, is a left-handed pitcher at the University of Michigan, who made the Big 10 All-Conference team last year. He sat out a year to rehab from an injury, but is scheduled to pitch again this year. He also is a pre-med major.

Taylor's other son is studying film and history at a university in Toronto.

"I didn't push them into baseball," Taylor said. "I let them decide what they wanted to do."

As for his own future, Taylor says he intends to keep working at least until he is 70 years old, then will most likely make a decision on how long he wants to continue working a year at a time.

"I will just have to see when I lose my marbles," he said, jokingly.

Where Have You Gone?

SCOTT TERRY

After spending two seasons working as a minor league pitching coach, Scott Terry decided he was spending too much time away from his family to make that job worth what he was being paid.

That didn't mean he was ready to end his time as a pitching instructor, however. He just needed to find a different audience.

For the last 10 years, Terry has made his living by offering private instructions to youngsters in the St. Louis area. He primarily works with pitchers but also teaches softball pitchers and has worked with catchers and other position players who want to improve their throwing technique.

He has taught kids starting as young as eight years old and has continued to work with some clients as old as 21, while they are pitching in college. Terry routinely works with 85 clients a week during the spring and summer and has as many as 60 students a week during the fall and winter months.

Terry also has a waiting list for openings that usually runs about 50 names deep at any given time.

When he isn't offering specific instructions, Terry talks, as often as he can to anybody who will listen, about what he thinks is wrong with youth sports in the U.S. today. Simply put, it is that kids are playing too many games with too much pressure on them at too young of an age.

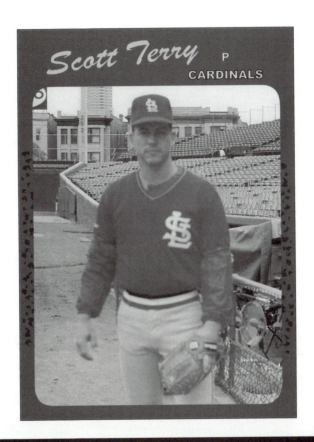

SCOTT TERRY
Seasons with Cardinals: 1987-1991

Best season with Cardinals: 1988

Games: 51 • Record: 9-6 • SV: 3 • ERA: 2.92 • IP: 129.3
Hits: 119 • SO: 65 • SV: 3

"I'm just one voice trying to talk as loud as I can," Terry said. "I don't know how much it's heard."

Terry thinks the biggest problem comes from the parents who make the mistake of telling their sons and daughters what they should do. Instead, Terry thinks the parents should simply allow the kids to play for fun and tell the parents what they want to do.

"I think too many parents try to relive their lives through their kids," Terry said. "They see dollar signs, and they push their kids to the limit and the extreme. They force kids to pick one sport and specialize on it at an early age and I think that's wrong.

"There are 10- and 11-year-old kids out there playing 80 baseball games in one summer, and I think that's wrong. I don't know too many kids that age who want to play baseball every day and never do anything else. I played a lot of baseball when I was that age, but they were just pickup games at the park. Nobody plays that way anymore; nobody has practice. They don't know the fundamentals as well, because all they are doing is playing organized games all the time."

The two kids Terry can be certain will listen to his advice and follow it are his own two sons, Cody, who is a sophomore at Oakville High School in St. Louis and Dallas, who is 12. Up until this year Cody has played football, basketball and baseball, but he is not playing basketball this season. Dallas is playing basketball and baseball and will add football to his list when he gets to the seventh grade next year.

"I just got so involved with my kids because it is so different now than when I was growing up in south Texas," Terry said. "They have all of the extra rules now, they don't really teach the game. Eight- and nine-year-old kids are stealing on every pitch, they are calling balks on the pitcher. I just couldn't understand why parents are asking so much of these kids at such a young age.

"Coaches will let a 10-year-old kid throw 100 pitches in five innings, then bring him back the next day to pitch two innings because they are trying to win a tournament and think nothing of it. That's wrong. My passion is to try to convince as many people as I can that kids should have the same opportunity to play the game for fun like I had."

If the number of clients he has is any indication, Terry's message is at least being received and accepted by more than a few people.

"I'm humbled and flattered by the number of kids who continue to come to me," he said. "We go at it four days a week in the winter and five days a week in the spring and summer. [I teach] between 60 and 85 kids all the time."

Before he made the major leagues, Terry earned his degree in education and received a teaching certificate, so he always thought his future would most likely be in teaching or coaching, especially if he didn't reach the majors.

Terry did pitch for six years in the majors, spending 1986 with Cincinnati and 1987 through 1991 with the Cardinals. He was used most often as a middle reliever but moved into the starting rotation for most of 1989. After his career, he was a minor league coach for Detroit and Texas for one season each before deciding he was not going to earn a fast promotion to the majors, and that meant the job was costing him too much money.

"This is kind of what I always thought I had a gift to do," he said. "One thing I am proud of is that I don't go out and recruit kids. We take anybody who wants to come to us, and they have to wait their turn until we have an opening. I am committed to what I teach. I think it is the right way."

About the only offer that would make Terry leave what he is doing now is a chance to become a pitching coach for a major league franchise. As much as he would like for that to happen, he is realistic enough to know it isn't likely to happen soon. So he will almost certainly keep doing what he is doing now for years to come.

"I have had various offers over the years for minor league jobs, but they weren't good enough to take me away from home," he said. "St. Louis is the only home my kids have known, and I don't foresee myself leaving anytime soon."

Where Have You Gone?

JOHN STUPER

Now in his 13th season as the head baseball coach at Yale University, John Stuper has had many great, enjoyable memories thanks to his job, like the time former president and former Yale baseball player George H. Bush dropped by for a visit. There also was one terrible, unforgettable day.

On the morning of January 17, 2003, an SUV carrying nine Yale students crashed into a jackknifed truck on an icy road. Four of the students were killed. Two of the four, Kyle Burnat and Nick Grass, were members of Stuper's team. The other two also had ties to Yale athletics.

"Without question, the hardest day of my life," Stuper said. "They were two of the finest young men I have ever had the honor to coach."

Not only did Stuper have to deal with the tragedy himself, he found the other members of his team looking to him for guidance, for solace, for the knowledge of how they were supposed to act.

Stuper said, "There is no chapter in the coaching manual for how to cope with the death of two of your players. You just try and take it a day at a time."

Stuper's team made it through that season, relying on each other for strength and comfort, and in 2004, despite having the youngest team he has had at Yale, the team went 19-20, including an 11-9 mark in the Ivy League.

CARDINALS
JOHN STUPER   PITCHER

JOHN STUPER
Seasons with Cardinals: 1982-1984

Best season with Cardinals: 1983

Games: **40** • Record: **12-11** • ERA: **3.68** • IP: **198**
Hits: **202** • SO: **81** • CG: **6** • SHO: **1**

He is excited about the team's chances in 2005.

"We basically return everybody and we still will probably only start one senior," he said. "They are real good guys, and we should be good for a while."

To say that Stuper enjoys coaching at Yale would be a great understatement. He was selected from a field of 120 applicants and hired in 1993 and has no plans to leave anytime soon. His wife, Pam, is the assistant field hockey coach for Yale, too.

"We've met a lot of great friends and we love it here," Stuper said. "We've kind of settled in. I don't want to ever get complacent, but it is a great situation for me."

All of Stuper's players were born after his brief four-year playing career in the major leagues came to an end in 1985. A rookie with the Cardinals in 1982, Stuper forever etched his name in the team's record book when he became only the 14th rookie in history to start two games in the World Series.

He won the rain-delayed Game 6 against the Brewers, which the Cardinals had to win to force a Game 7. Some people suggested that was the night Stuper hurt his shoulder, coming back after long rain delays. The injury eventually cut short his playing career, but Stuper doesn't believe that game caused the injury.

"It probably didn't help that I pitched that game," Stuper said. "I found out later the problem was I had a really weak shoulder."

Stuper started 21 games for the Cardinals as a 25-year-old rookie in 1982, going 9-7. He pitched well again the following year, winning 12 games, before his shoulder trouble began to worsen. He was sent back to the minors in 1984, then traded to the Reds.

He spent the 1985 season in Cincinnati, winning eight games, then was traded to Montreal. When he was asked by the Expos to begin the 1986 season in Triple A, primarily so they could cut his salary, Stuper refused and instead retired.

Less than a month later he was hired as the baseball coach at his alma mater, Butler County Community College in Pennsylvania. He also spent two years working as a pitching coach in the Cardinals' farm system before getting the job at Yale.

"I regret that I didn't get to pitch longer, but I crammed a lot of good things into three years," Stuper said. "I got to pitch in the

World Series and I got a ring. It took me a couple of years to get over it. I would see a guy pitching on television and say, 'I know I'm better than that guy.' You just have to cope with whatever is thrown your way."

Playing for Whitey Herzog and Pete Rose, his manager with the Reds, helped make Stuper a better coach. He tries to use many of the lessons they taught him every day, even though he works in a much different environment than major league baseball.

According to Stuper, there are unique challenges to being the coach at Yale, compared to coaching at other more traditional baseball schools. He understands and embraces those differences. Primarily, he has to be more concerned with a high school student's academic record when he is recruiting a player than is often the case at other schools.

"Batting average and height and weight is not the first thing I look at," Stuper said. "I know if they can't do the job in the classroom, they are not going to be admitted into Yale. We go to all of the same showcases around the country as the other schools, we are just there looking at different kids. We can't bring in junior college kids to give us a quick fix, and we can't offer money. But we offer a Yale education. We get great kids."

His relationship with his players is right at the top of what Stuper enjoys the most about coaching at Yale, which is why the deaths of two of his players were so difficult for him to overcome.

"If I have ever taken this job for granted, I never will again," Stuper wrote in an article published in *The Sporting News* six weeks after the two players were killed. "I am a lucky man to have known and coached Kyle and Nick. My life has been made richer because of it."

Stuper has a goal as the coach at Yale that he honestly believes will be realized one day. It is not to win the national championship. Stuper wants to one day pick up the telephone and call the White House, and when they find out who is calling, put his call right through to the President of the United States, because he used to play for Stuper in college.

He still doesn't know, of course, who that future president will be, but he has one strong candidate at the moment.

"I'm not going to tell you who he is. He's in his last year at Harvard Law School," Stuper said. "He's my top candidate right now. We'll see what happens."

Where Have You Gone?

PHIL GAGLIANO

The reality of life after baseball for his generation became very apparent to Phil Gagliano when he finished his 12-year career with the Cincinnati Reds in 1974.

"I was 32 years old with four kids, and I had to get a job," said Gagliano, who had kept his home in St. Louis even after leaving the Cardinals. "I had to make the adjustment, like everybody. The biggest adjustment was financial. I went from making $40,000 to $16,000 a year. I was starting all over again, and I was 10 years behind.

"I had given 15 years of my life to one profession and then it was over, and I was only 32. Some guys were able to make the adjustment and became very successful in their life after baseball. Some people can't ever make the adjustment. It took me a good five years of adjustment to get baseball out of my blood."

Unlike today, the money earned by most players from his era was not enough to set them up for life, Gagliano says. A player who lasts 10 years in the majors today should never have to worry about working another day in his life if he has been careful with his money.

But, players in the '60s also had to work separate jobs during the off season so they would have money to pay their bills. That is another change in the game today.

Gagliano is not jealous or envious of today's players. He knows he was lucky to play 10 years in the major leagues and he appreciates

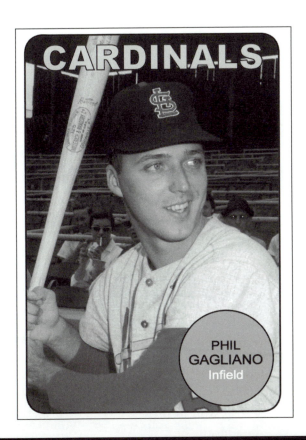

PHIL GAGLIANO
Seasons with Cardinals: 1963-1970

Best season with Cardinals: 1965

Games: 122 • At-bats: 363 • BA: .240 • HR: 8 • RBI: 53 • R: 46

what he received from baseball. He also was glad that he was lucky enough to find a good job that he enjoyed after his playing days were over.

For two years Gagliano worked as a sales rep for Paramount Liquor and then went to work for Durbin Durko, Inc., an industrial hardware manufacturer. He started out as a salesman then moved into management and finished his 17 years with the company as its operations manager.

Gagliano retired two years ago and he and his wife, Betty, moved to the small southwest Missouri town of Hollister, not far from Branson, after living in St. Louis since 1969. That has been another adjustment, he says.

"We got a letter in the mail talking about some land down there so we went down there and checked it out and really liked it and decided to move," Gagliano said. "It's really country living. In the summer I play a lot of golf and the kids all come and visit. I don't do much of anything in the winter."

Gagliano has four children and nine grandchildren. Two of his children still live in the St. Louis area, one in Kansas City and one in Alabama.

Gagliano began his career by playing in 10 games for the Cardinals in 1963 and stayed in St. Louis until 1970, when he was traded to the Cubs. He experienced the best season of his career in 1965, when the backup infielder played a career-high 122 games and hit eight homers while driving in 53 runs.

The 63-year-old Gagliano also played in the 1967 and 1968 World Series, and still proudly wears his 1967 World Championship ring.

"Those were the best memories," he said. "It was a great team and a great bunch of guys."

After playing for the Cubs for less than a year, Gagliano spent two years in Boston and two years in Cincinnati before retiring. Because of his connection to both the Cardinals and Red Sox, he watched the 2004 World Series a little more intently than normal.

"Both are great baseball towns," he said. "It was a great postseason. I wish the Cardinals had played a little better in the World Series."

Gagliano returns to St. Louis often to visit his family and also to make appearances at Cardinals events, such as the Cardinals' annual winter warmup in January, where he sits and signs autographs for two hours.

"It's just amazing how these people still know who you are and appreciate the fact that you played on the Cardinals and what you did back then," he said. "It puts a smile on your face and makes you feel good."

Where Have You Gone?

BOB SYKES

A couple of years after he had left the Cardinals and then retired from baseball, lefthanded pitcher Bob Sykes was back at Busch Stadium, in the locker room visiting with some of his friends. He went over to Willie McGee's locker and congratulated him on his success and wished him well in the future, saying, "You're my ticket to the Hall of Fame."

"He had no idea who I was," Sykes said, "so I told him: 'If you make the Hall of Fame, I will be there too. On your plaque it will say '…traded for Bob Sykes on October 21, 1981.'"

There was a time when Sykes was uncomfortable with the fact that the only thing he is remembered for in his career was that he was traded for McGee, at the time an unknown minor-leaguer in the Yankees system. As he has grown older, and more removed from the moment, however, that feeling has changed.

McGee had his first year of eligibility for the Hall of Fame in 2005 and received enough votes to remain on the ballot next year, but faces long odds of ever being elected. Whether he actually does get voted into Cooperstown or not, however, will not change Sykes's opinion of McGee.

"Willie is so humble and shy and he is a great player, but better than that he is a great human being," Sykes said. "A lot of people ask me what my greatest day in baseball was, and I really think it might

CARDINALS
BOB SYKES

PITCHER

BOB SYKES
Seasons with Cardinals: 1979-1981

Best season with Cardinals: 1980

Games: 27 • Record: 6-10 • **ERA: 4.64** • **IP: 126** • **Hits: 134**
SO: 50 • **CG: 4** • SHO: 3 (fourth in NL)

have been when the Cardinals invited me to come back and be part of Willie McGee Day when he was retiring."

At the time of the trade, Sykes was more upset simply to be leaving the Cardinals. It didn't matter where he was traded to or whom he was traded for.

"I had a no-trade clause in my contract and in the middle of the season they asked me if I would give my permission to be traded to the Yankees," Sykes said. "I wouldn't give it to them. I said I would rather finish the season in St. Louis.

"On the last day of the season we were in Pittsburgh and Whitey Herzog called me into his office and said, 'You know you are not going to be in a Cardinal uniform next year.' I knew it, but I still didn't like it. St. Louis was the greatest place in the world to play. I knew I was going to be traded, I just didn't know where."

The trade became so lopsided when McGee turned into a star with the Cardinals that it made Yankees owner George Steinbrenner upset; he believed that he had been taken in the deal. The Cardinals ended up basically giving the Yankees two more minor league prospects, including Stan Javier, to try to even up the deal, even though they had no requirement to do so.

Sykes had been traded to the Cardinals by the Tigers after the 1978 season and pitched in St. Louis for three seasons, combining for a 12-13 record as both a starter and reliever.

He was in the minors for the Yankees in 1982, and was released out of spring training in 1983. He debated whether to try to hook on with another club, and actually participated in a tryout camp with Atlanta, which was looking for a left-handed reliever.

"I went, but my heart wasn't really in it," Sykes said. "I realized that [my baseball career] had come to an end."

Sykes was only 29 years old and hadn't given much thought to what he would do when he was out of baseball.

"I had never dreamed of anything else," he said. "I didn't think about what I would do when I was done playing. I doubt if most players think about it."

Sykes returned to his wife Jane's hometown of Carmi, Illinois, about two hours east of St. Louis. The couple had met in Evansville, Indiana, when Sykes was pitching there for Detroit.

After going through the culture shock of being an ex-player, Sykes went to work for the Tartan Oil Co. and has been there ever since. He has now moved into more of an administrative position.

In addition to that full-time job, Sykes, who is now 50, has been running a baseball school at night for the past several years, drawing kids from the mostly rural part of the state.

Sykes tried to de-emphasize his life as a former major leaguer for years, believing it was important that he become involved in his community, not because of the fact he had played in the majors but for his own personal abilities.

"I wanted people to like me for who I was and who I am, not for what I did," Sykes said. "It was important for me to become a part of the community for reasons that had nothing to do with what I did. That has worked out well."

Sykes, who has two grown children, says the highlight of his actual playing career was getting a chance to play for Herzog for his three years with the Cardinals.

"Every major league player should be lucky enough to get a chance to play for a guy like Whitey," Sykes said. "He could take 25 guys who are so different and make them into a team. He had the ability to take the 25th guy on the team who was barely hanging on and make him feel special, like he was the best guy on the team. That's a special talent that not many people have."

Where Have You Gone?

TITO LANDRUM

A doctor's appointment might have saved Tito Landrum's life on the morning of September 11, 2001.

Landrum, who now prefers to go by his given first name of Terry instead of Tito, was working at the time as a physical therapist for a company, Plus One, whose offices were in the American Express building in Manhattan, adjacent to the World Trade Center.

If Landrum had been working that morning instead of seeing a doctor, he would have likely been in the office when the terrorist planes struck the Twin Towers. Even though no one in his office was killed, Landrum never will know what would have happened to him if he had been there.

"Everybody down there was thinking about trying to help other people," said Landrum, who knows he might have been one of the people who ran into the building trying to help lead people to safety. "It was just a horrifying experience.

"By the grace of God, I had a doctor's appointment. I came out of the office and saw all the ruckus."

Like everybody in New York, Landrum's life changed that day. He no longer takes so many things for granted, and he values life more. "I have a greater appreciation and understanding that we are here for a short period of time," he said. "I'm not walking around corners blindly anymore. It matured me."

TITO LANDRUM
Seasons with Cardinals: 1980-1983; 1984-1987

Best season with Cardinals: 1985

Games: 85 • At-bats: 161 • BA: .280 • OBP: .356
HR: 4 • RBI: 21 • R: 21

Landrum has been living in New York since his baseball career ended in 1992. A woman he had met in St. Louis, Carol Williams, had accepted a job for ABC in New York and Landrum moved there with her. He really had no idea what he was going to do but finally decided to take on the challenge of going back to school.

At age 39, Landrum enrolled at New York University having only attended part of one semester at a junior college when he was 18. Four years after entering NYU, he earned his degree in physical therapy. Even though other students had higher grade point averages, Landrum was selected by his classmates to deliver the valedictorian speech during the graduation ceremonies at Carnegie Hall.

"When I started college in my late 30s, I was more frightened than I had been in my entire life," Landrum said in his speech. "I was surrounded by teenagers, really smart teenagers, teenagers who had been studying while I was watching my former career evaporate. When you stop being a professional baseball player, you suddenly remember that no one told you what to do next. And I had no idea what to do.

"Somehow I pushed down the fear and tried one class. It felt like my first day in A ball, except when I was in the minors I was the same age as my teammates. But I got through it. And I kept going. …I spent eight long years in the minors, and then I made it to three World Series. Not one of them felt as good as it feels to be here today."

Landrum, who is now 50 years old, had two stints with the Cardinals, from 1980 through 1983, and again from 1984 through 1987. He was not on the World Series roster in 1982, but was called upon in a big way in the 1985 World Series. Because of the injury that kept Vince Coleman from playing against the Royals, Landrum started all seven games and was one of the few Cardinals who did well offensively, hitting .360. He also played a huge role in helping the team make it to the Series, collecting six hits and driving in four runs against the Dodgers in the NLCS.

Landrum played for the Dodgers in 1987 and Baltimore in 1988 before finishing his career in the minor leagues.

Perhaps his most famous moment in uniform came while playing for Baltimore in 1983. His 10th-inning home run in Game 4 of the

ALCS against the White Sox helped the Orioles win the pennant and send them on to the World Series, where they defeated the Phillies.

Landrum does not dwell on those baseball experiences very much these days, preferring to concentrate on his new life as a physical therapist. He lost his job after the 9-11 attacks when Plus One was forced to lay off people as it moved to a new, smaller office. Landrum worked independently for a while, then went back to Plus One, but now has joined a new company, Ice, which will offer physical therapy services to athletes and professional entertainers in the New York area.

The company was started by two trainers from the New York Knicks, and among its first clients are the NBA referees.

"These guys have a lot more experience and knowledge than I do and I am looking forward to learning from them," Landrum said about moving to the new company. "I went on three different interviews, and during the last one, the man who was interviewing me said, 'I read an article on you when you were going to NYU. I knew your resume would pass my desk someday.'"

The new company will put Landrum into contact with many orthopedic doctors in the New York area, as well as professional and up-and-coming athletes from all sports, and people in the entertainment industry.

Landrum has not been surprised by how much he enjoys being a physical therapist. Having been injured numerous times during his baseball career, and having gone through rehabilitation, he knew what the requirements of the job would be.

"I knew I was going to like it, but I didn't know to what extent," he said. "I had been through the rehab process, and I know what an athlete has to go through to try to get back on the field. I knew I was going to be able to help a lot of people, and seeing them get back playing has been a great experience. I know all about the low points you go through in the process, and I think I have been able to help them get through it."

Where Have You Gone?

CHARLIE JAMES

Most baseball players whose career ends when they are 27 years old likely find themselves in a dilemma about what to do for the rest of their life. Not Charlie James. When his career ended three months shy of his 28th birthday in 1965, he knew exactly what he was going to do.

"I had an electrical engineering degree from Washington University in St. Louis, so I always knew when I was done playing I would go to work," James said. "I had three interviews and the best offer was from Bussmann Manufacturing in St. Louis, so that was where I went. They made electrical fuses."

James, who grew up in the St. Louis suburb of Webster Groves, spent five years there before an opportunity came up to buy into Central Electric Co. in Fulton, Missouri. The company manufactures electrical power equipment for industries.

When James became president of the company in 1972, it had annual sales of $1 million. When he retired in 1998, the company had grown to $22 million in annual sales. It is safe to say he had a much more successful career after he retired from baseball.

"It's kind of hard to compare," said James, who also earned a master's degree from Washington U. "I do think my experience competing in baseball helped me prepare for the competition in business. When I left baseball I probably didn't think I would get involved in

CHARLIE JAMES
Seasons with Cardinals: 1960-1964

Best season with Cardinals: 1962

Games: 129 • At-bats: 388 • **BA: .276** • HR: 8 • **RBI: 59** • R: 50

the ownership of a business. I expected to be working for somebody else for a period of time, probably in sales or something.

"When we made the decision to move up here, I figured we would probably be here quite a while, but I never realized we would be here the rest of my working life."

One unusual fact about the 1964 Cardinals is that three of the players on the team—James, Dal Maxvill and Ron Taylor—all had earned college degrees in electrical engineering. James, who finished his degree by attending one semester of classes for three years while he was playing, was the only one of the three to go into that line of work after his playing career ended. Maxvill stayed in baseball and Taylor became a doctor after also going to medical school.

James, now 67, is still involved in numerous community activities. He also enjoys spending time with his family, which includes his wife, Jo, his son and daughter and five grandchildren. His daughter lives in Fulton and teaches at William Woods College, and his son lives in Columbia and teaches at the University of Missouri. James also is an avid golfer and spends time hunting and fishing.

James has many fond memories of his baseball career, which began when he joined his hometown Cardinals in 1960. He played with the Cardinals through 1964, then was traded to Cincinnati with pitcher Roger Craig for pitcher Bob Purkey. He played 26 games for the Reds in 1965 before retiring.

His top career highlight came when he hit a grand slam off Dodgers Hall of Famer Sandy Koufax.

"That was a big thrill," he said. "You couldn't hit Koufax's 100 mph fastball, but if the ball started at the knees, it would rise to belt high by the time it got to the plate. That was the only way you could hit it."

Even though he spent the game sitting on the bench, James says the most enjoyable moment in his career was the final day of the 1964 regular season, when the Cardinals beat the Mets to clinch the pennant and a spot in the World Series against the Yankees.

He received his most playing time during the 1962 and 1963 seasons. In 1962, he hit eight homers, drove in 59 runs and hit .276. The following year, James hit 10 homers, drove in 45 runs and hit .268.

James was the starting leftfielder for much of the first half of the 1964 season, then went back into a reserve role when the trade was made with the Cubs that brought Lou Brock to St. Louis.

Even though the deal affected his playing time, James knows the Cardinals likely would not have won the pennant without Brock's contributions.

"Having grown up in St. Louis as a fan of the Cardinals, it was a nice honor to have a chance to play for my hometown team," James said. "St. Louis was a great organization then and is still a great organization today."

Where Have You Gone?

GARRY TEMPLETON

There was no question Garry Templeton was an extremely talented player. He led the Cardinals in hits for three consecutive years from 1977 to 1979, including a league-leading total of 211 in 1979. He became one of the few switch-hitters in history to record 100 or more hits from each side of the plate in the same season. He led the team in triples for four consecutive years, three times leading the league, and even had two years in which he led the Cardinals in stolen bases.

Templeton was a two-time All-Star with the Cardinals, but despite all of that talent, Manager Whitey Herzog was convinced he was not a player he wanted to build his team around. When he had the chance to trade Templeton to the Padres for Ozzie Smith he jumped on the deal, not even imagining that Smith would turn out to be a Hall of Famer and one of the greatest shortstops in history.

Herzog valued Templeton as a very good player, and since he was trading a shortstop, he needed to obtain a shortstop in return. The only other shortstops he considered near equals of Templeton were Smith, Rick Burleson of the Red Sox, Alan Trammell of the Tigers and Ivan DeJesus of the Cubs. When he learned that Burleson,

GARRY TEMPLETON
Seasons with Cardinals: 1976-1981

Best season with Cardinals: 1979 (All-Star)

Games: 154 • At-bats: .672 (third in NL) • BA: .314 (sixth in NL)
H: 211 (first in NL) • 2B: 32 • 3B: 19 (first in NL) • HR: 9 • RBI: 62
R: 105 (sixth in NL) • SB: 26 • Total bases: 308 (seventh in NL)

Trammell and DeJesus were not available, he set his sights on Smith, who had experienced his own run-ins with management in San Diego. The deal was struck to send Templeton, Sixto Lezcano and a player to be named later to the Padres for Smith, Steve Mura and a player to be named later.

Most of the Cardinals fans who remember the Garry Templeton who left St. Louis after his very public meltdown in 1981 would be surprised to know that he has been managing in the minor leagues for six of the past seven years.

Templeton himself finds that a little surprising—for a different reason.

Templeton believes he could be an effective manager in the major leagues if he were given that opportunity. He doubts if it will ever happen, however, and he is probably right.

Instead of working in a major league stadium, Templeton spent the past two seasons managing the Southshore RailCats, a team from Gary, Indiana, that plays in the independent Northern League. While the league is doing well financially with new, elaborate stadiums and increasing attendance, the league is not traditionally a steppingstone for managers aiming for a higher level.

There were three former major league managers working in the Northern League in 2004, but none of the three—Tim Johnson in Lincoln, Doc Edwards in Sioux Falls or Hal Lanier in Winnipeg—is likely to manage at that level again in the future.

Templeton especially is going to have trouble finding a team willing to invest in him after his struggles of the past two years. The RailCats were the worst team in the league in 2004, finishing with a 31-65 record, and for his two seasons in Gary, Templeton's teams had a combined record of 67-119.

Prior to moving to Gary, Templeton spent four years managing in the Anaheim Angels farm system, between 1998 and 2001, including two years in Triple-A. Many of the players who were part of the Angels' world championship team in 2002 played for Templeton at some point in the minor leagues.

Templeton said he left the Angels when the team made a change in its player development front office. After spending a year out of baseball, he was excited about the chance to manage in Gary.

It turned out to be a harder assignment than he expected, however, because of the level of baseball, and because with an independent team, the manager also has to play a role in acquiring players, not just managing them.

"When you are working for an organization you can teach kids and work with them and let them grow," Templeton said. "Here the only thing that counts is winning. I'm more of a teacher. That is what I consider my strength. I have more fun working with the younger kids."

Many of the players Templeton is working with, or has worked with in the past, probably don't remember him as a player. If they do, it most certainly would be for his years in San Diego, not his years in St. Louis.

Templeton is one of the minority of players who does not look back too fondly on his years in St. Louis. He declines to discuss much of what happened with the Cardinals, except for the biggest regret he says he has about his playing career.

"I should never have let them talk me into becoming a switch-hitter," Templeton said. "I should have been a right-handed hitter my entire career. I think I could have achieved more."

As far as his personal problems that existed with the Cardinals, including his Ladies Day display at Busch Stadium, where he made a series of obscene gestures to the crowd and had to be pulled into the dugout by Herzog, all Templeton will say is "I was young and made some mistakes."

The 48-year-old Templeton, who now has a great deal of gray in his hair color, had a good career with San Diego, but believes he never was as good as he could have been because of seven operations on his left knee, which robbed him of much of his speed on offense and his range on defense.

One of Templeton's two sons played in the Northern League in 2003. He has anther son and two daughters, ranging in age from 19 to 30.

Despite not returning to Gary for the 2005 season, Templeton still sees his future in baseball.

"I think I have a lot to offer kids," Templeton said. "I knew going to Gary was going to be a challenge, and it just didn't work out."

DAVE LAPOINT

L ike many other former players before him, Dave LaPoint didn't know exactly what he was getting himself into when he accepted a job to become the pitching coach of an independent minor league baseball team, the Long Island Ducks of the Atlantic League, in 2002.

"I really thought it was going to be a one-year stopover," LaPoint said. "I had been managing, and I really wanted to get back into that. It turned out to be such a great place that I've stayed."

LaPoint, a Cardinal from 1981 to 1984 and then briefly again in 1987, has added a new title to go along with being the team's pitching coach. He is the director of player procurement, meaning he is in charge of finding and signing players for the club, which is not affiliated with any major league organization.

It has been easier to find players since the Ducks won the league championship last year.

"This is really a great place, once you figure out the traffic pattern," LaPoint said. "We are 40 minutes from Manhattan, and the league basically surrounds New York City. There are more former major leaguers in our league than in all the other leagues except Triple-A. Ex-major leaguers involved in managing or coaching include Sparky Lyle, Bill Madlock and Butch Hobson. Dante Bichette and Henry Rodriguez played in the league in 2003. The

CARDINALS PITCHER
DAVE LaPOINT

DAVE LaPOINT
Seasons with Cardinals: 1981-1984; 1987

Best season with Cardinals: 1984

Games: 33 • Record: 12-10 • **ERA: 3.96** • IP: 193 • **Hits: 205**
SO: 130 • **CG: 2** • SHO: 1

minority owner of LaPoint's team is former Mets player and manager Bud Harrelson.

LaPoint, 45, is not surprised that he is still working in baseball. Other than a brief period in which he owned and operated a restaurant and bar in his hometown of Glens Falls, New York, he has been involved in baseball in some capacity ever since he retired as a player after the 1991 season. He even spent two years working as a pitching coach for the Cardinals Double-A farm team in 2000 and 2001.

The years he spent playing for the Cardinals were definitely the best years of his career, LaPoint says. Traded from Milwaukee in the deal that sent Pete Vuckovich, Rollie Fingers and Ted Simmons to the Brewers, LaPoint moved into the St. Louis rotation as a 23-year-old rookie in 1982.

LaPoint started 21 games for the world championship team, going 9-3, and also started Game 4 of the World Series. He was involved in the key play in that game, when he dropped a throw covering first base in the bottom of the seventh inning. The Cardinals were leading 5-1 at the time, but the error helped the Brewers put together a six-run inning which gave them a 7-5 victory, evening the World Series at two wins each.

LaPoint's only regret about the inning is that he would have liked to have had a chance to pitch around the error, instead of turning the game over to the bullpen.

Usually that move worked during LaPoint's tenure with the Cardinals. He won 35 games as a Cardinal, and Bruce Sutter saved 33 of them.

"If you got the hitter to hit a ground ball he was out," LaPoint said. "If you had a lead in the seventh inning, you won. How great was that? Those were the things that made it easier."

LaPoint won 12 games in each of the 1983 and 1984 seasons, then experienced what he calls the toughest day of his career when he was part of a package traded to the Giants for Jack Clark before the 1985 season.

That began an odyssey that took LaPoint to eight different teams over the next seven years. Among his few highlights was returning to St. Louis as a member of the Giants and pitching a 5-0 shutout over the Cardinals, which earned him a standing ovation from the fans in Busch Stadium.

LaPoint won more than 10 games in a season only once after leaving the Cardinals, in 1988, when he won 10 games for the White Sox and four more after he was traded to Pittsburgh. In his career, he also pitched for the Tigers, Padres, Brewers, Yankees and Phillies, compiling an overall record of 80-86.

Looking back on his career, LaPoint is disappointed that he moved so quickly through so many organizations, but he also now knows why. The reason is something he didn't know or didn't realize at the time.

"I was wild and talked too much," he said. "I just wish someone along the way had taken me aside and said, 'Hey.' Maybe they did and I didn't notice."

LaPoint has had challenges in his personal life as well, being divorced twice. His two sons from his first marriage are now 21 and 17, and he finally had a chance to bring them back to St. Louis with him when he appeared at the Cardinals' winter warmup in January 2005.

"They couldn't believe it, all of these people standing in line for my autograph," LaPoint said. "I tried to tell them. There is no place like St. Louis."

One job LaPoint has not had in baseball, which he thought would have been a natural for him, was broadcasting or at least hosting a talk show. For whatever reason, it has never happened.

"I found out announcers die less frequently than baseball players," LaPoint said. "There weren't that many job openings. It's like anything else—I didn't know the right people. I thought I knew everybody, but I guess we weren't that good of friends."

DICK GROAT

A couple of generations of fans of the University of Pittsburgh basketball team have grown up thinking of Dick Groat as the analyst on the radio broadcasts of the team's games, not as a former baseball player.

The 2004-2005 season marks Groat's 26th year of working with Bill Hargrove on the Panthers' broadcasts, a job he truly enjoys. Now 74 years old, he has no intentions of slowing down anytime soon.

"I enjoy the game and I enjoy the kids," Groat said. "They help keep me young."

In truth, Groat always preferred the game of basketball to baseball. He played both sports at Duke University and was a two-time All-America in basketball in 1951 and 1952. As a six-foot guard, he was the team's leading scorer both seasons, averaging 25 points a game in 1951 and 26 points and seven assists a game in 1952.

Groat was a first-round draft pick of the Fort Wayne Pistons of the NBA that season and played one year with the team, appearing in 26 games and averaging 11.9 points a game.

Groat was forced to make a decision after that season, however, when he signed with the Pittsburgh Pirates and team boss Branch Rickey refused to let him continue to play both sports. Groat chose baseball, and went on to a long and successful career.

"I was a much better basketball player than I was a baseball player," Groat said. "It was always my first love."

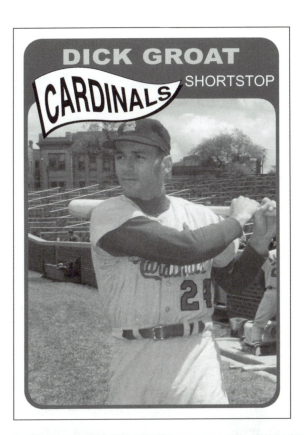

DICK GROAT
Seasons with Cardinals: 1963-1965

Best season with Cardinals: 1963 (All-Star, second in NL MVP voting)

Games: 158 • At-bats: 631 (fifth in NL) • **BA: .319 (third in NL)**
OBP: .377 (fifth in NL) • **SLG: .450** • H: 201 (second in NL)
2B: 43 (first in NL) • 3B: 11 (third in NL) • **HR: 6** • RBI: 73 • **R: 85**

He was also a good enough baseball player, however, to be named the NL's MVP in 1960 with the Pirates and to enjoy a career in the majors that lasted from 1952 through 1967. He was a five-time All-Star.

Included in that career was three years as the Cardinals' shortstop, from 1963 through 1965. The Cardinals acquired Groat from the Pirates after the 1962 season in a trade involving Julio Gotay and Don Cardwell. Groat actually had a much better statistical year in 1963 with the Cardinals than he did in 1960, when he helped the Pirates win the World Series and was named MVP. In 1963 he led the NL with 46 doubles, hit 11 triples and six homers, drove in 73 runs and posted a .319 average. In 1960, he led the league with a .325 average, but the rest of his production was below his 1963 numbers.

"The three happiest years of my baseball career were spent in St. Louis," Groat said. "The Cardinal organization, owned by Mr. Busch at the time, was absolutely wonderful to me. It was a first-class organization in every possible way. And the people in St. Louis treated me great."

Groat had an easy explanation for his success in 1963—"I was hitting in front of Stan Musial all year."

Even though his numbers declined the following year, Groat was a key player in the Cardinals' collective success, winning the pennant and beating the Yankees in the World Series.

The Cardinals traded Groat to the Phillies after the 1965 season, along with Bill White and Bob Uecker, in exchange for Pat Corrales, Art Mahaffey and Alex Johnson.

On Christmas Eve of 1964, Groat and partner Jerry Lynch, a former Pirate teammate, broke ground on a golf course in Ligonier, Pennsylvania, about 60 miles east of his hometown of Pittsburgh. The Champion Lakes Golf Course opened the day after the 1966 season ended. Groat and Lynch are still partners in the facility, ranked by *Golf Digest* as one of the best public courses in western Pennsylvania.

From May through September, Groat lives in a home on the golf course and works there full time.

"Neither of us had a great desire to stay in baseball and we decided to build a golf course," Groat said. "Right now it's a terrible business to be in because there is an over-saturation of golf courses everywhere. I've always enjoyed playing golf, and probably played more last summer than I had in the last eight to 10 years."

While he was getting the golf course up and running, Groat also spent 17 years working as a national sales rep for Jessup Steel Co., working in the winter while he was still playing and then working there full-time for several years after his playing career ended in 1967.

One of the big differences between baseball then and now, Groat says, was that players then had to work other jobs in order to stay financially afloat; they were not able to retire and live off their savings.

Groat is still a baseball fan and is active in the Pirates' alumni association, which annually raises about $1 million for charity. He also enjoys watching his five grandsons and one granddaughter play a variety of sports. He has three grown daughters, two of whom live in the Pittsburgh area and one who lives in North Carolina.

Where Have You Gone?

TODD WORRELL

The secret to happiness in Todd Worrell's post-baseball life is a piece of advice his father gave to him when he was growing up, many years ago.

"My dad was always a firm believer in not letting any one thing dominate your life," Worrell said. "You have to have balance."

For Worrell, that balance allows him to spend time with his wife, Jaime, and their four children, perform a variety of duties for the Fellowship of Christian Athletes (FCA) on both a local and national level, and operate a hunting lodge in South Dakota.

The one piece of his life that Worrell had no idea he would be doing when he retired after the 1997 season was owning and operating a hunting lodge, located 20 miles west of Mitchell, South Dakota.

Growing up in southern California, Worrell was not much of a hunter as a youngster. He developed the bug after joining the Cardinals, where the opportunity to do a variety of hunting was much more readily available. When a friend invited him to go pheasant hunting in South Dakota, he immediately was hooked.

"I probably went up there just to hunt for close to 10 years, and got to know a lot of people," Worrell said. "Finally I told them that if they knew of anybody selling land I would be interested. I thought it would be neat to put a home there for my family to enjoy.

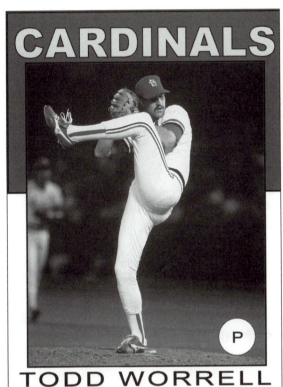

Focus on Sport/Getty Images

CARDINALS

TODD WORRELL

P

TODD WORRELL
Seasons with Cardinals: 1985-1992

Best season with Cardinals: 1986
(NL Rookie-of-the-Year, NL Rolaids Relief Award)

Games: 74 (third in NL) • Record: 9-10 • ERA: 2.08 • IP: 103.7
Hits: 86 • SO: 73 • SV: 36 (first in NL)
Games finished: 60 (first in NL)

"I got the opportunity to buy 1,500 acres and it all just came together. It really became a hobby, and instead of just building a house we decided to open a hunting lodge. It became a small business. My dad and I spent two summers building the lodge and we opened it in 2001."

The business has been much more popular and successful than Worrell could have imagined. He organizes and runs eight weekend hunts a year during the pheasant season, which runs from October through December. He also organizes two hunts as fundraising events for the FCA.

Each hunt has a maximum of 13 people, and Worrell accompanies each group with three other guides. All of the hunters stay at the 7,000-square foot lodge.

"Ninety-five percent of our business is recurring business," Worrell said. "You know that if you give up a weekend you are not going to get it back. It really is a hands-on experience. A lot of people just put out the birds and turn the people lose. Not a lot of lodges do what I am doing.

"We provide the habitat and the food and we guarantee that we will not overhunt our fields. We have a meeting the night before and go over all of the safety issues. We are very strict about safety."

Worrell even established a Web site for his lodge and hunts at www.firesteelcreek.com.

When he is running one of the hunts, Worrell flies back and forth twice a week between South Dakota and his home in St. Louis. That again provides him with that outside balance in his life.

In the spring, Worrell spends his time working as the pitching coach at Westminster High School, where his son Joshua is a senior and son Jeremy is a sophomore. His third son, Jacob, is in eighth grade and daughter Hanna is in the sixth grade.

"I've been doing that for four years now, and I really enjoy it," Worrell said. "I work with the younger kids as well as the older ones. Andy Benes has been helping me the last couple of years."

All of those kids are too young to remember much of Worrell's prime with the Cardinals, which came in the mid- to late 1980s. He was converted from a starter into a closer at Triple A and was called up in August of 1985 as the Cardinals were battling the Mets for the division title.

He took over the closer's role and helped the Cardinals into the World Series, where he was involved in perhaps the most infamous play in team history, the blown call by first base umpire Don Denkinger in the ninth inning of Game 6. Worrell received the throw from Jack Clark and stepped on first base ahead of Jorge Orta. But Denkinger ruled that Worrell missed the base—even though Orta actually stepped on Worrell's foot—and called Orta safe.

The Cardinals were ahead 1-0 at the time, three outs away from the world championship, but the Royals took advantage of the opening to rally and win the game 2-1, setting the stage for the debacle in Game 7.

Worrell remained the Cardinals' closer through 1989, leading the league with 36 saves in 1986 and earning the Rookie of the Year award. He missed the 1990 and 1991 seasons because of injuries, came back and pitched well in 1992 for St. Louis and then signed as a free agent with the Dodgers.

He spent the last five seasons of his career in Los Angeles, retiring after 1997 with a career total of 256 saves.

Even though Worrell didn't know specifically what he would be doing in retirement, just as important was his knowledge of what he wouldn't be doing.

"I had a lot of interests to pursue," he said. "I was surprised by how many guys came up to me and wanted to know what it was like to be out of the game. I hate using the word retired. They thought all I did was play golf every day.

"I think it would drive you nuts if all you had to do was play golf every day. I would get bored after two months. I was lucky I got some good advice early and was able to cultivate my interests. I have no trouble staying busy.

"I miss the competitive part of the game. There is nothing that can really replace that. But I have found other passions, other things I enjoy. Luckily baseball provided me with those opportunities."

Celebrate the Heroes of Cardinals and St. Louis Sports
in These Other Books from Sports Publishing!

Albert the Great:
The Albert Pujols Story
by Rob Rains

- 8.5 x 11 hardcover
- 128 pages
- color photos throughout
- $19.95

St. Louis Sports Folks
by Tom Wheatley

- 6 x 9 hardcover
- 250 pages
- black and white photos
- $22.95

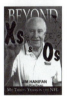

Beyond Xs & Os:
My Thirty Years in the NFL
by Jim Hanifan
with Rob Rains

- 6 x 9 hardcover
- 250 pages
- black and white photo section
- $22.95

A Special Season: Players'
Reflections on an Inspiring
Year
by Rob Rains

- 6 x 9 hardcover
- 250 pages
- black and white photo section
- $22.95

Jack Buck:
Forever a Winner
by Carole, Joe, and Julie Buck

- 8.5 x 11 hardcover
- 144 pages
- color photos throughout
- $24.95 • (2003 release)

Red: A Baseball Life
by Red Schoendienst
with Rob Rains

- 6 x 9 hardcover
- 218 pages
- black and white photo section
- $22.95

The Memoirs of Bing
Devine: Stealing Lou
Brock and Other Winning
Moves by a Master GM
by Bing Devine
with Tom Wheatley

- 6 x 9 hardcover • 184 pages
- photo insert • $24.95

Ozzie Smith:
The Road to Cooperstown
by Ozzie Smith with Rob Rains

- 8.5 x 11 hardcover
- 128 pages
- photos throughout
- $24.95
- Leatherbound Edition, signed
  by Ozzie Smith: $49.95!

Bob Forsch's Tales from
the Cardinals Dugout
by Bob Forsch
with Tom Wheatley

- 5.5 x 8.25 hardcover
- 200 pages
- photos throughout
- $19.95

Tales from the Blues Bench
by Bob Plager
with Tom Wheatley

- 5.5 x 8.25 hardcover
- 200 pages
- photos throughout
- $19.95

All books are available in bookstores everywhere!
Order 24-hours-a-day by calling toll-free **1-877-424-BOOK (2665)**.
Also order online at **www.SportsPublishingLLC.com**.